How Can
I Keep
From Singing

By Kittie Preas Koukalik

ISBN-13: 978-1508970170

ISBN-10: 1508970173

Printed in the United States of America

DEDICATION

When I asked God "why are you doing this?"
He answered "Not doing this, allowing this"

When I screamed "I can't live if you take him!"
He would answer "I am what sustains you".

When I prayed "let this cup pass from my lips".
He said "pray for what is best for him".

When I begged on my knees "heal him, make him well".
He said "all things work for good for those who love me".

When I held his still body and sobbed "it's over".
He said "It has only begun".

When I asked Him "WHY?"
He answered "slowly... you will heal and comfort others".

(author unknown)

"This is the purpose for this book!

I dedicate it to my precious Terry, who taught me to love and was the love of my life, but also to my amazing Tommy, who taught me that I could love again, and is the love of my SECOND life!"

~~ Kittie

How Can I Keep From Singing

By Kittie Preas Koukalik

If you want to make God laugh, tell Him what you have planned for the day

He always awoke early, at least by 4:30 or 5:00 a.m. He enjoyed his coffee and alone time, to watch the news, plan his day and collect his thoughts. I, on the other hand slept in most mornings since the kids had left home some years back. I usually woke up about 7:00 a.m.

This was Wednesday, his tenth day into a tank job at the greenhouse. Usually he did not disturb me, but this morning his intentional stirrings woke me up and he held me in a snuggle, which was unlike him. He teased me about an early morning "urge" he had, but then laughed it off with that quick wit that defined him so well. After telling me he loved me, Terry got up as I turned over to go back to sleep. It was some time later that I heard his vehicle start and he rode off to his tank-building job, just about ten minutes from our rural home.

I had no way of knowing that this was the last time I would see him alive or that my life, as I knew it, was over.

Terry and I had met by chance when we lived in Texas. It was Christmas Day 1970. I had just turned 17 and he was 18, we were both still in high school. He lived in Ft. Worth. I lived in a tiny town about 175 miles away. He said he went home the night he met me and told his mom, that he had met the girl he was going to marry. I teased him for years, telling him that he was awfully sure of himself!

Our long distance romance moved quickly. He told me he loved me on the first date.

Terry came to see me every weekend, we wrote every day, and soon after he graduated, we married on July 2, 1971. I finished school that next year while he made minimum wage at a sheet metal shop. This job, though, would teach him much and would be the driving force to his love of working with metal.

In July of 1973, we decided to take up an offer to move to the Willcox, Arizona area.

Terry wanted a better life for us, and what seemed like a lot of money then, would be nothing now, but a lot more than he was making at the sheet metal shop. When we arrived here, Terry told me we had arrived at "the promised land". He loved Arizona, the mountains, the climate, the irrigated farming, as well as the challenge of a new life.

He went to work as a farmhand and even though he was only 20 years old, he gained the respect of the farmers he worked for during the ten years that followed, and was the farm manager for some of the biggest farms in the valley. This would teach him even more and give him credibility for his work ethics when eventually, in 1982, he started Preas Welding.

Terry during his young farming years in the Bonita Valley

In 1980 we had built a home in the Bonita area, I was working at the Prison and we had two children. There was a very small shop that was on the property when we built the house.

It was no secret that I thought Terry was crazy when one morning he woke up and told me he had had a dream. In this dream he was to start a welding business. He had, to my knowledge, little experience as a welder, only had a small cracker box welder and furthermore, how on earth do you run a welding business 27 miles from town?

So several years later he would laugh and tell friends that he started Preas Welding with "$40.00 and a mad wife". In my mind, with two chronically ill kids, the last thing we needed was to be self-employed.

But Preas Welding was born in April 1982 and succeed, it did. With every industry that came to the valley, we jumped on board, whether it was planting apple and peach trees, building planting equipment, ostrich buildings, pistachio plants, chili plants and equipment, farm and ranch equipment and/or general repair. He also became the maintenance person for the local grain elevators. Anything that needed to be built or repaired, Terry was called on to do so, not only because of his work ethics, but his ability to visualize something in his mind and then build it. One of the biggest farmers in the Bonita Valley once said Terry was "more like an artist than a welder when he picked up that welding stinger".

Terry also became well known for his western metal art, known as silhouettes or "cut outs". He used a cutting torch and with a free hand, cut out western scenes like a cowboy on a horse with a calf trailing behind or a coyote howling, and then cut the person's name on it. Those pieces of work can still be seen hanging on and in homes in the area. They were sold more than just locally, made and donated for raffle donations, not to mention gifts that he made for his special friends at Christmas. My job during all of this growing business was bookkeeping, dispatching jobs, answering the phones, typing bids and contracts, cooking for hired men, going for parts or materials. Oh how I loved that welder I was married to!

Terry was also known for having friends in for deer and javelina hunts. When he met someone he hit it off with, he would say "come on down and hunt with me". They usually would and this would be the beginning of even more lasting friendships. He had English Pointer bird dogs and loved to quail hunt on afternoons he could sneak off work early. As Terry went into what he didn't know would be the final years of his life, hunting was replaced with a love for fishing for flat head catfish.

He bought a used pontoon boat and stored it at Roosevelt Lake. Every available weekend, he could be found sitting on his boat "The Drownin' Worms" not only fishing, but also visiting with God. A man of great faith, Terry loved sitting on a rock somewhere in the mountains, just listening to the peace and talking with God. While he attended church at one time, he said he could find much more of God in the hills, lakes and mountains God had created than he could in most churches.

Sometimes, he would meet his cousin Wilber at Roosevelt and they would fish together. They became as close as brothers while catching flat heads weighing as much as 65 pounds. When the weather wasn't too disagreeable, I would go fishing with him. You see, when you fished with Terry, "The Drownin' Worms" was also the campsite. We would arrive at the lake on Friday about lunch and we slept, ate, camped, fished and cooked on the boat until Sunday morning.

I loved those times and still cherish the memories of them! I recall fishing for crappie at night and watching the stars, hearing the fish flounce while the boat gently rocked with the motion of the water. When I was ready to go to sleep, Terry would make my "bed" up at the back of the boat, get me into my sleeping bags and tuck me in.

Terry with some of his large fish caught at Roosevelt Lake

I would lie there and watch the beautiful star lit sky and feel the boat rocking on the water.

I was with my darling…I knew I was safe.

If fishing was good, we would be awakened at night by the reels sounding as the big flat head zoomed off with the bait. We would both jump up with excitement, and he would start tightening the reel, patiently bringing the fish in, while I would grab the gaff or net and be ready as he got the fish in close to the edge of the boat. The first time I saw him reel in a 42 pound flathead, I immediately shared his love of catching these big fish. With the dawn of a new day, I would wake to the smell of freshly brewed coffee and my fisherman Terry would bring a steaming cup to me. He would cook a camp breakfast for us on the boat and then we would wash up the dishes and start another day. If it got too hot for me to fish, I would retire to my "bed" and read.

It was so peaceful for us, no phones, and only the sounds of nature. I was with the man I loved more than anyone else in the world. When the weather got too hot for me to go, I would stay behind and I remember him standing at the back door telling me goodbye, always saying "I love you and if something happens to me, I will meet you on the other side where the river forks."

Terry also enjoyed his Wednesday night low stakes poker club.

It consisted of several local men who were offended if they lost ten bucks! When he left, he would say, "I'll be home early if I'm winning and late if I'm losing". This meant that if he was winning, everyone folded and went home. Terry enjoyed this night out so much that he often said, "I only miss poker in the event of a death....mine". He was killed on a Wednesday.

In the mid 80's, most of our springtime work came from irrigation plumbing.

Terry spent four months of the summer in 1987 in Yuma, Arizona working for a large citrus company, completely revamping all of their irrigation systems. He also did irrigation plumbing all across the valley and into New Mexico.

In 1984, he had purchased another acre adjoining our home property and built a 3000 sq. ft. shop. There became a demand for Terry to build buildings so in 1994 we became Preas Welding & Construction. He built many large buildings all over the area to include an indoor roping arena for the Merry Star Ranch in Sonoita, Az. He also did some work for the Santa Cruz County Fair, more buildings. Robert Barnhill, the owner of the Merry Star, hired Terry to build horse fence all around a large part of their Arabian Horse Ranch. He spent a lot of time between 1982 and 1989 working at the Merry Star. He would stay there in the stable hand's apartment. My job was to raise the kids, take care of business locally, and do whatever else he needed me to do, while still keeping my job at the Prison Post Office. Terry would say later that "going to the Merry Star was like visiting a 'Preas Welding Museum". This is what birthed our company logo "We weld anything 'cept the crack of dawn, the break of day or a broken heart".

Terry serviced the local grain elevators as well and in the last few years of his life, actually built three-grain elevators for local farmers.

Terry was known for his outstanding work on all of his jobs. For the years he owned the business, I photographed and videotaped many of his jobs to chronicle the work done when a similar job came along. It was exciting to go back through the history of his work. Never in all his years of welding, did Terry ever have a weld break! He found it rewarding to teach the young men who were drawn to him, and they were eager to work with him, and be taught by "the master of the best" as they put it. While he was a patient teacher, he never tolerated sloth or inferior workmanship. If his company name was to be on a job, then it would meet his standards or it would be redone and the young man who had not done it properly would be coached fully before doing it to the standard expected. Each of these young men became fine welders and considered it a privilege to have Terry teach them the trade that he so loved.

Two of these young men would be welding inside the tank on the day of the accident.

Fate? Perhaps.

His motto with them was "asses and elbows, boys!" which meant he didn't want to see anything but their elbows and butts in the air, with their heads down as they worked.

This saying later became a joke among the men when on his 50th birthday; he was given a gift with that saying engraved on it.

But friendship is the breathing rose...with sweets in every fold
Oliver Wendell Holmes

Eurofresh had come to our Bonita valley in 1992. They came from the Netherlands to build a multi-acre hydroponics greenhouse for growing tomatoes. This area was chosen because of its sunshine and excellent ground water. Some valley residents were not excited about this new venture, but for Preas Welding, it meant jobs.

Later there would be another Dutch man who would build a small family owned greenhouse in the same area. This man, Jacque Van Der Lilij hired Terry on many projects in the construction of the "Willcox Greenhouse". In addition to a horizontal water tank, one of these projects was three massive stainless steel water tanks 22,000 and 18,000 gallons to hold oxygenated water from Jacque's and another man's own invention. Jacque and Terry became very close friends.

Terry took great pride in everything he built for Eurofresh and for the greenhouses in general. He was so impressed with the concept of growing tomatoes without soil, he would take visitors for tours of the facility and show off the uniqueness of the business, and introduce them to all the friends he had made with the Dutch. We often invited the Dutch guys into our home, celebrated with cookouts, and had barbeques and fish fry's with them. We also enjoyed taking them to see many places of interest in the Bonita area. This was the beginning of a friendship and business relationship that would last for eleven years. Terry had by now, become the "right-hand man" at Eurofresh, and as always, he took great pride in this. He had built, with his own crew, 10 or more tanks for Eurofresh, both horizontal and upright.

By 2000, Eurofresh, for financial reasons, had begun bringing in their own men to do the actual welding. Their names were "Koos" and "Ton", (pronounced KOSE and TAWN). Koos was an older man with a quick wit and sense of humor while Ton was younger and more serious. The three of them became great friends. These two men not only taught Terry on a previous Eurofresh/Bonita job, but they taught him the Dutch way of constructing water tanks. The first job they worked on was in the spring of 2000. Upon the completion of this job, Terry wrote them this letter.

"June 1, 2000
Dear Koos and Ton,

I have been in the welding and tank business for most of my adult life and would like to say it's been a great honor for me to work with men like you! Your skill and knowledge is unparalleled, not to mention your sense of humor, work ethics, and just plain, real, no nonsense approach to "get the job done". Life for me has always been like a big college. I learn something new every day. Education costs money and time, so I am paying a small installment to each of you for "advanced tank construction". I believe the way you build tanks will become the standard way in this country, in the near future, for its speed and safety alone. I know I will use this method to advance my company. So I thank you two for the education!

Friends for life…

With love and respect,
Terry Preas"

With this letter he enclosed a check for $800.00 for each of them out of his pay for this job. How odd was it that a subcontractor would give a bonus to two men that worked for another company, because of the things he had learned from them! But that was my husband!

Over the years with our sick kids, we had fallen on hard times and people had stepped forward to help us.

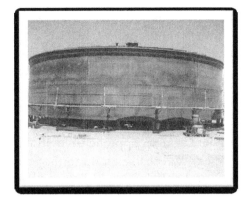

The tank he was killed in, just days prior

It was very hard for this proud man of mine to accept help, but he knew he had to for the sake of our children, so his philosophy would become "pay it forward". If Terry had any faults, it was that he was too good, too giving, which at times, allowed him to be taken advantage of. But he continued, "paying it forward", and it kept "coming back". Our company website had his comment "the harder I work, the more I am blessed".

In the spring of 2002, Eurofresh purchased a small greenhouse in Snowflake, Arizona. They hired Terry and his crane to go to Snowflake and "fly" or "swing" the steel for the construction of a huge water boiler tank, at least a half million gallons.

The Snowflake tank job was the second one Terry had done with Koos and Ton. He loved working with them. Their skill was indeed unparalleled and the friendship was one that would last until Terry's untimely death. We had a crew working at our shop, and I stayed there for most of the week to do my office duties and make payroll. Every Friday, I was off to Snowflake to see my honey. I would return on Monday morning, but not before I visited the tank site and took pictures. This continued for five weeks until the job was done.

In May 2003, Eurofresh/Bonita was constructing "Site 4" which would be a total of 170 acres under glass.

Terry had been very ill with herniated discs in his back from September through December 2002 and we had been forced to close our business and live on our savings while he recovered. So when the offer to help construct the tank on site 4 was extended, Terry was excited for the money and also for the opportunity to work once again with his good friends Koos and Ton.

As fate would have it, in the early planning stages and negotiation of the contract, he learned that Koos and Ton would not be making this trip. Koos had broken his leg and Ton was having family issues, and they would not be coming. Instead, the Dutch company would be sending two other men to do the welding. Almost immediately, apprehension began to build in my husband. He always rented all of his welding machines to this crew of welders and as he and I began to move equipment over to site 4, his concern about this job became more apparent. He had an unexplained uneasiness. He was nervous and worried. I recall him telling me that this was the last tank job he would be taking. He said "let me do this one and replace our savings and then I won't do anymore". I asked him "Why are you so apprehensive about this job? You have done this so many times!" We chalked it up to the fact that Koos and Ton would not be there and that he would be working with new people.

This project began on the 18th of May. They worked ten-hour days, six days a week.

Some days I would go over and sit in the shade with him to visit while he ate his lunch.

He always wanted to show me the progress and introduce me to people.

As with the two previous tanks, Terry and his crane were hired to "fly" the steel, set it in place, and then the Dutch welders would tack weld it to hold it into place. With the help of some local welders, including some who had worked for Terry at one time, they would construct the tank one sheet at a time, one ring at a time, and as the rings went on, it would be lifted from the bottom, so that in fact, there would be about a three or four foot crawl space at the bottom.

The completed dimensions for these tanks would be approximately 54 feet tall and 50 feet in diameter, and it would sit on a concrete slab. The design of this tank utilized three circular steel plates, spaced at different elevations inside the tank, for the purpose of diffusing the flow of incoming hot water. For this process, "diffuser plates" were placed at the top of the enclosed tank. Each of the plates was 16 feet in diameter, 1/4-inch thick steel and weighed 1600 pounds. Although a number of tanks had previously been erected at Eurofresh, this is the first tank that used diffuser plates. The three diffuser plates for this tank had been fabricated and welded on one side. Two of the three plates were then "spot welded" together so they could both be hoisted and turned or flipped over at one time. This had been done a week or so earlier by the Arizona welding crew which had been hired by Eurofresh.

The fabrication, welding one side, and spot welding two diffuser plates together, was done inside the tank after the roof was in place. The fact that the roof and several sections of the tank wall had already been completed combined with the fact that the diffuser plates had to be flipped over while inside the tank, meant that the crane's ball and hook would not fit through the small opening at the point of the roof. This meant that the crane operator would not be able to see the load, or the workmen, or the work being done inside the tank during the hoisting, flipping and lowering of the plates, if he was to remain safely on the crane. Eurofresh did not provide a ground spotter. That crane operator was my husband, Terry who had done no welding on this job.

The crew of welders was hired by and was under the supervision of a man named Marcos Juarez. Mr. Juarez held no license and only had a lay person's welding skills. Terry told me this man was paid $20.00 an hour to coordinate the building of the tank and to hire and supervise the welders.

Mr. Juarez was the person on the job site responsible for making the decisions regarding when the diffuser plates would be fabricated, welded, flipped, and who was to perform each task. He was also the person who would determine the method and the means of rigging and flipping the diffuser plates. He would direct and supervise each procedure. Marcos made the decision to use "Ears" or "Eye Plates" welded to the face of the diffuser plates as attachment points for the rigging strap used in the lifting of the plate. All of the welders inside the tank stated that they had not seen Terry welding any of the eye plates or "ears". However, no one could say who had done the welding. It was determined that the welding had been done the week before.

The "ears" had circles roughly cut in them using a cutting torch. For this procedure, Terry would have punched the holes, using his "pride and joy" machine, a big Piranha Iron Worker.

Marcos decided the morning of May 28, to flip the diffuser plates. However, he would not be on site, since he was working in another area. Terry had completed his duties so offered to flip the plates. Marcos agreed to let him, and provided him with two young men to help, one of whom could not speak English.

Marcos left the tank to attend to his other duties. He left Terry with two inexperienced helpers but no separate rigger and no lift supervisor or ground spotter to help while Terry was operating the crane through the hole. Since there was no one to supervise the work from inside the tank,

Terry had to leave the crane during the hoisting of the load to go inside the tank and check to make sure there was clearance to start the flip procedure. At that time, one of the ear welds failed, which caused the full load of steel plates to drop inside the tank, directly where Terry stood. He was unfortunately in the path of 3200 pounds of steel, which fell on him and crushed him.

The scene of the death, with his bloody shirt and the steel that fell on him

Statements would later say the welders inside the tank heard a loud CRASH and turned to see a cloud of dust. It fact, the crash was so loud, as one could only imagine, that the Sheriff's Report later stated that he was called to a "fire of undetermined type" in one of the tanks at Eurofresh site 4, because they thought it was an explosion.

The time of that call was 11:40 a.m. The Deputy also said that while he was in route to the scene, he was notified to get the helicopter on its way for a medical emergency. EMT's came from both Willcox and from the local prison about ten miles away.

Statements also showed that as soon as the dust cleared, the men welding inside the tank realized that Terry was under the 3200 pounds of steel and together they somehow managed to "pry" the steel off Terry as someone pulled him out. Two of these welders were men who had worked for Terry and were friends of his.

That day I had started a 27-mile drive into Willcox. On the way, instead of making my usual route down past Eurofresh, I took an alternative route.

On the way, my cell phone rang.

It was Terry. It was about 9:40 a.m. He told me that he was going to the shop by the house to meet the steel truck that was making a weekly delivery.

He ended the call with his usual "I love you".

I had an appointment after which I dropped a friend off and made my way toward the greenhouse. As was my usual routine, I had planned to stop by the job site, camera in hand, to take photos. In fact, I had done so just a few days earlier, on Saturday.

A security pass was required to get into Eurofresh and I had a tag hanging on my windshield. I thought nothing of it as I went through the gate and the security person raised the bar and I drove through, making my way to site 4, and around back where the tank was being constructed. Upon my arrival there, I saw an ambulance parked by the tank. There were workers standing around and I could tell by the way people were looking at me that something had happened to Terry.

My heart began to race as I ran over to the area where the ambulance was parked.

I was immediately intercepted by one of our Dutch friends, Jan (pronounced Yan) who told me that Terry had been injured. In his strong Dutch brogue, I thought he said a piece of steel had fallen on Terry's HAND, but he said the paramedics were inside the tank with him. I immediately got on my knees and crawled through the small space at the bottom of the tank. Terry was about to be put on a backboard by paramedics. I ran over to his right side and grabbed his hand and said "I'm here" and then I moved back to let the paramedics do their work. Terry's screams told me how badly he was injured as they got him onto the backboard. He began to have a seizure. Jan was standing there with me and I screamed "he's seizing!" and then Jan pulled my face back into his chest, and told me not to look. I stood there. My knees were weak and shaking and I knew this was serious. Terry had been injured on jobs before but nothing like this. I was not focusing on my surroundings and didn't notice the enormous steel plates lying beside my husband, or his shirt lying in puddles of his blood. All I saw was his battered body and the paramedics.

After he started seizing, they moved him into the ambulance to transport him 25 miles into Willcox. Although Jan told me that someone would drive me to the hospital, I ran to my truck and drove myself. When I arrived at the hospital I realized that the ambulance had never passed me. I went immediately to the outpatient clinic area and asked the person in charge what had happened to the ambulance that had been dispatched to Eurofresh. She asked me to take a seat while she checked.

In what seemed like an eternity, but I am sure now was only a minute or two, she returned and told me that the ambulance "wasn't coming". I panicked and began to scream, "he's dead, he's dead!" as I turned and raced out of the hospital lobby and headed frantically back toward the job site.

It was just a mile or two down the road that I called Eurofresh again and was told that the "chopper had arrived" and that someone would be there to take me to the hospital in Tucson. I insisted that it would be faster for me to drive myself. I gave the secretary my cell phone number as I turned around and headed toward Tucson, which was nearly 100 miles away. I called our son in Tucson and told him what was happening. Our daughter was attending a trade school and he went to get her out of class. I received a call later that the two of them would meet me at the hospital in Tucson. I was driving as fast as I could but the truck's computer kept shutting it down at 100 mph.

I don't know who all called or whom I called, but I do know from later cell records that there were a total of seventy-two phone calls on my cell phone that day.

One of the first people I called was my Mom in Texas.

She began to call family, and my family was then calling me.

Strangely I had purchased a plane ticket a few days before to fly out to see her on Friday, May 30.

She had been ill for some time and had recently suffered congestive heart failure.

On the Monday night prior to the accident on Wednesday, Terry and I were talking about me visiting my mom, and out of the blue he said to me "If something happens to me, don't hold my ashes, scatter them at the falls".

The day of the accident, driving to Tucson, one of the many phone calls I received was from one of my sisters in Texas. She said, "Kit, I called Eurofresh and they said the chopper hadn't left". I immediately called the girl I had been in contact with—a precious young girl named Amy, and asked her what was going on.

She said "they can't get him stable enough to load him into the chopper". I knew we were in trouble. I asked Amy if I should turn around and head back or if I should go on to the hospital. She told me that she couldn't make that decision for me. I hesitated and finally told her I would head back, so I did an illegal turn in a median about twenty miles out of Tucson and headed back. I was in such a panic; I really should not have been driving.

Terry always said to watch what you pray for and I knew this was serious, and so I didn't pray, "let him live," but rather "Lord, let him be okay".

At some point in the nightmare, I made contact with my nephew in Willcox who had law enforcement contacts. He had already been informed that this accident was very serious, so he told me he would meet me at the truck stop in Willcox and drive me to the site. I stopped just long enough at the roadway to meet up with him and we proceeded back to the site. He also discovered the truck shut off at 100 mph. What seemed like an eternity later, we pulled into site 4 at Eurofresh. The helicopter was gone but I didn't notice the ambulance still sitting there. My nephew asked the deputy and some other men standing near the tank "where did they take Terry?" The deputy slowly walked over to the truck, and came to the passenger side where I was sitting.

When he spoke, I heard the words I will never forget and never thought I would hear.... "Kittie, I am sorry but Terry passed away".

I could only scream "NO, NO, NO, NO!" Several people tried to console and comfort me, to hold me up but my world went black, and in a split second I went from a wife to a widow!

How could it be that he was dead? I had just had lunch with him here a few days ago. I had just spoken with him on the phone a few hours earlier. It couldn't be true, it just couldn't. But it was. My precious husband, my best friend, was gone.

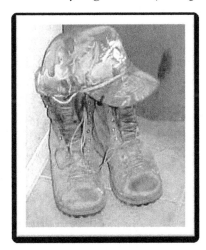

His boots and hat that he was wearing when he was killed

The ambulance was still there and I desperately needed to go to Terry. I asked the deputy if I could go inside and be with Terry. He told me I could not, because the county coroner was in route from Safford, just about an hour and a half away. Since it was an industrial accident, he said it was against the law for me to touch the "body" until the coroner arrived. I begged! I screamed, "Please let me in, he shouldn't be alone! I won't touch anything, I just want to be with him and hold his hand!" He still

21

refused. Even though he was a big man, I tried to push past him to be with Terry. They restrained me, threatening to arrest me if I persisted. At that moment, I hated him.

This man would later testify that this was not a law, but rather a decision he and one of the paramedics had agreed on. They chose not let me in until the coroner was done. I sat and cried and waited.... and waited and cried. I looked at the ambulance and could just imagine my darlin' lying in there alone. We were sweethearts; we were "joined at the hip", he needed me and I had let him down. I never got to say goodbye.

While we were waiting, the agonizing phone call came from our daughter. She and our son had arrived at the hospital in Willcox, only to find their dad was not there. I had no choice, but to tell her the truth. I said "Becca, your dad died". She cried and cried. She was her daddy's girl! I heard our son scream, "I hate God".

I understood.

We agreed that they needed to come to the job site immediately so they could say "goodbye" to their dad before the ambulance had to take his body away.

Finally the Coroner arrived. He did the necessary things in the ambulance and then came to me and told me we could go in. My nephew, who loved Terry very much, went with me. We inadvertently opened the rear door to the ambulance and the first thing we saw was Terry's work boots!

We were redirected to the side door, opened it and went in. The events of that day and what I saw when I got into the ambulance will forever be etched in my memory. The engine was running and the air conditioner was on. There was his body, on a gurney, covered with a bloody sheet. As I pulled back the sheet, I saw him ...my darlin' husband, my very best friend, my childhood sweetheart. There were tubes in his mouth, blood all over his broken body. I took his hand from underneath the bloody sheet.... it was so soft. I kissed it. I closed his sweet, gentle eyes, and kissed them. I kissed his face. I lay over his battered body as I wept and told him goodbye.

I didn't want to leave him. The paramedics needed to take him, but our children had not yet arrived. They needed to say goodbye to their Dad. Soon, they did arrive. There was not enough time it seemed.

Our daughter Becca was a tower of strength that day, while our son begged for more time with his Dad. He wept. My daughter wept. I wept.

The tears seemed to flow from a river that would flow for a long, long time. This had to be a dream, a nightmare. He couldn't be gone! He just couldn't! Didn't God, in His infinite wisdom, know that I needed Terry more than He ever could? This just couldn't be happening. It just couldn't be! As I got into my truck, I happened to look up just in time to see Terry's body, covered in a sheet, being moved from the ambulance to the coroner's vehicle. As they drove away with his body, I recall my daughter saying, "let's go home." How could I go home? Part of me had just been taken away. How could I ever go home?

No one ever told me that grief felt so like fear
C.S. Lewis

My nephew drove me home and the kids followed. As we pulled in the shop yard, there were about a dozen men, neighbors, and friends already at the house. Word of Terry's death had spread like wildfire and people were already there, offering comfort, asking what they could do to help. The next few hours are dim. There were phone calls, many calls, to be made. The house was full of people from all over who had come to pay their respects. People immediately began to bring food, so much food. I stayed in the office for the most part, on the phone, or looking through photos.

As I recall, that first night, it was just the kids and I. Becca slept with me, and I slept on Terry's side of the bed with one of the tee shirts that he had worn. His smell was fresh and I smelled it all night. The next morning I awoke and thought the whole thing had been a nightmare, but when I realized it wasn't, I cried so many tears once again.

The next day was even more a blur. How could it be? The house was still full of people, and everyone was offering to do what they could. People were in and out but I was either tearful or oblivious as I stayed in the office on the phone.

My sister Karen had lost her husband of 42 years only four months earlier. He was found dead on his fishing boat of an apparent stroke. Terry said "what a way to go!"

How I wish Terry could have gone that way, instead of the violent way he died. The death of my brother in law had a strange effect on me. I couldn't shake the fear of going through what she had, facing the death of my husband, being alone. I recall going to see a counselor in March that I had seen many times in the last 14 years or so.

She told me later that I must have had a "premonition". Terry had said to me "Kit, you worry so much about me dying that you can't enjoy me living" After the accident, my family was preparing to come, all four of my sisters, with my mom and her companion. I had told Karen I wanted her son, Kevin, who is a pastor, and one of my favorite nephews to come and do Terry's service. He was a Pastor at a church in Oklahoma, but one phone call, and he said he would be there. Thursday night, my daughter Becca slept next to me. I was, that night, awaiting the arrival of my family, and so I slept on the couch, Becca on the floor beside me. I remember her waking me in the night, her crying, "Daddy, please come back!"

About daybreak, my family arrived from Ft. Worth Texas. My mom had been released from the hospital after congestive heart failure a few days earlier. She was 87 years old.

She made the long trip, 17 hours, sitting up in a seat of the van, oxygen and all.

Nothing could have kept her away.

Terry's mom didn't want to make the two-hour flight for her son's service. I didn't understand it. I needed her. Her grandchildren needed her and yet she didn't come. The only ones of his family that came was his brother, one sister in law, an elderly aunt, and his niece and her husband. This was a small representation, considering the size of his family. It was very hard for us, because at a time like this, we needed his family, my family and our friends. Less than two years earlier, Terry's mom had made a road trip of over 12 hours for her daughter's funeral. In respect for her, I will say that Terry was the 6th child she had lost and maybe she felt she just couldn't do it anymore. But we still needed her. It hurt me deeply.

I now had to call Terry's cousin and fishing partner, Wilber, to tell him that Terry was dead. Wilber had lost all four of his brothers to cancer, and though Wilber lived in Phoenix, they had become as close as brothers in the previous years because they spent so much time together fishing. Wilber came immediately. His heart was so broken!

I was in touch with the mortuary about the memorial service but could never get together on any plans. When my nephew, Kevin arrived on Friday, he said, "If you are just having a memorial service you don't have to work with the mortuary." I knew I had to decide on a time. The local elementary school had offered the gymnasium, as they often did for services. I knew that this was the place to have it. I finally set the date for Saturday, May 31. Word spread as people called and information was also put on the signboard at the school and the mortuary.

Because I did not want the cremation done in Willcox, the mortician agreed to transport Terry's body to Sierra Vista, about 75 miles away. He would then bring the ashes back to Willcox. Meanwhile Terry's family and I had been in touch by phone and they asked about a private family viewing. Terry's body had to be sent to Tucson for an autopsy, required by OSHA. The body was sent to Tucson for the autopsy and was to return on Friday morning to Willcox. His family was to be in on Friday after lunch, so I set up a viewing for Friday evening.

This would turn out to be a tragic mistake! As wonderful as the mortician was, he did not warn against this, or give any details to prepare us for what we would see. Naively, I called that afternoon and asked if we could bring in a western shirt to have him put on Terry before the family saw him. He said yes.

The afternoon came and a friend and I went into the Mortuary, ahead of the family, as I had to take care of the financial arrangements. Our friend, I will call Dick, went in to see the body before I did. Dick returned and told me "Don't go back there Kittie, it isn't our Terry."

But I felt as though I had to.

The family arrived at the mortuary. Some of the family did not want to view his body but were just there for support. My sister Karen was one that did not want to. She would tell me later "When I heard your blood curdling screams, I knew I was right about not going". She also told me later that our son Scott came out at one time, drenched with sweat and in tears, saying to his sister "you lied, you lied". She had told him it would make him feel better to see their dad. We had to sign a waiver if we were going to view his body. This should have been a warning to us all. Terry's entire body, everywhere that had been cut in the autopsy, was draped and covered. There was no need for a western shirt, though they had put it on him, it was not visible because of the draping. Even his head was draped, leaving only his face showing. His face.... oh his face…it was massively swollen, huge, from the trauma. He looked nothing like himself, nothing at all. When I saw him was when my sister had heard the "blood curdling scream". I had to go and sit down in the chapel at one point. I heard the wheels of my mom's oxygen cart, as she was coming into the room and I said "Mother, don't look".

But Mother looked. My Mother was a strong woman, having suffered her own losses and she loved Terry like a son.

I don't know how long we were there. It seemed like an eternity. I wished I had never gone, that we had never done the viewing, that someone had warned me. I wished so very many things.

As we got in vehicles to drive away I told Dick I needed a drink. He went to the local convenience store and bought 7-Up and vodka. I hadn't eaten at all since the accident and the doctor had prescribed Valium. Within a few minutes I was numb, I didn't have to feel any pain.

I was told later that it took three people to get my drunken, limp body into the house and into my bed. I don't recall anything. I just knew that I wanted to escape. I wanted to escape from the reality that the other half of me was gone, and was never coming back. I wanted to forget what I had seen at the death site and at the mortuary!

That Fateful Morning

"That fateful morning we said goodbye, I never dreamed that you would die. You are my life, my love, my friend; I never thought our time would end. I would have held you close to me, had I but known what was to be. The anguish of my broken heart, the knowledge that we must part. Seeing you lying there, so quiet and still, I thought to exercise my will, and call you back, to keep you near, it was not to be, that much was clear. Your soul had flown to God above, who holds you close in His true love. Those of us left below must turn you loose and let you go."

After Kevin's arrival, we had briefly discussed plans for the service. We decided to finalize the plans after the viewing. I had given him a list of songs and some things I wanted read. However, since I had numbed the pain with alcohol, I was unable to do so. Saturday morning came. It was the day of the service and I had not made any decisions. When I told Kevin I was sorry, his reply was "Don't worry, Jesus and I have it all worked out."

At some point after the viewing, my sisters and a dear friend, Joni, had been working diligently making photo boards and other things to arrange magnificent memorial tables for the service. I don't know what I would have done without these angels, as the results were outstanding. I didn't know for eight months who drove me to Terry's service. I learned then that it was our dear friend Mike. I was shocked when we arrived at the gymnasium to find virtually no parking available and people lined up all the way to the outside road. Somehow I got into the building. Music was playing. I had asked to have mine and Terry's favorite "sleeping" music play while the people were filing into the building and making their way to their seats.

The music was by ENYA. His favorite song of all her songs was called "How Can I Keep From Singing." I found out later that it was a very old gospel song.

The words were as follows:

My life goes on in endless song above earth's lamentations;
I hear the real, though far-off hymn that hails a new creation.
Through all the tumult and the strife I hear its music ringing, it sounds an echo in my soul.
How can I keep from singing?

While though the tempest loudly roars, I hear the truth, it liveth.
And though the darkness 'round me close, songs in the night it giveth.
No storm can shake my inmost calm, while to that rock I'm clinging.
Since love is lord of heaven and earth how can I keep from singing?

When tyrants tremble in their fear and hear their death knell ringing,
when friends rejoice both far and near how can I keep from singing?

In prison cell and dungeon vile our thoughts to them are winging,
when friends by shame are undefiled how can I keep from singing?"

The cars outside in the parking lot were far too many to count. As I walked into the gymnasium, I couldn't believe the number of people who had come to show how much they loved my husband; over 550 signed the guest book. Somehow I made my way inside. The first thing I saw was the table in the front with beautiful flowers and on the table was

Terry's Stetson hat, one of his camouflaged company caps, some of his metal artwork and other memorabilia. I folded! Was this all that was left of my darlin'?

I found my way to a seat, surrounded by our kids. In a few minutes, my nephew Kevin, knelt down in front of me and whispered "Aunt Kittie, the service is due to start in about ten minutes and people are still lined up all the way to the street outside!" It was then that I turned to look at all the people in the gymnasium. We decided that he would request that people come in and take a seat, and sign the guest book later, so that we could get started. After some time, the service began with a welcome, the obituary, songs, including a tape recording of our Becca singing "Daddy's Hands". So many people were crying. The principle of the school had set up a video recorder and was taping the service for me.

Kevin opened the microphone for those who wanted to pay tribute, and many did over the next hour or more. They spoke about how Terry was a "fixer of machines and men"…how he had touched their lives. Ironically, the eulogy was about how Terry had left many structures in the community but mostly how he had left his "footprints." Kevin commented about the people in the room were the people Terry had invested in.

Someone read "The Village Blacksmith", a very fitting poem. Though I had not planned to do so, I decided to take the microphone. I spoke of the way Terry and I met, about our love, our very special love. I would be told later "when you stood up and spoke, there wasn't a dry eye in the place, and everyone there left with an admiration and a new understanding for the love you and Terry had". I ended with the fact that he had died trying to help someone else.

The eulogy was from Rev. 1:12-18. Kevin spoke about how Terry had stepped from this life, through death's door into Heaven and had seen the bright face of God. If I could have been comforted, it would have helped to hear these words, but I was consumed with grief!

After the service, people came to the house and I recall so many flowers, flowers everywhere, in both living rooms, and all along the front porch. People were everywhere. I was standing on the front porch that bright sunny day, when suddenly, and very briefly, the sky turned dark and there was a fleeting shower of rain, which left as quickly as it had come. It was as though Terry was letting us know that he had made it and was watching over us that day.

Death leaves a heartache that no one can heal, love leaves a memory no one can steal

The days ran together. It was time for my family to return to Texas. My kids had already gone back to Tucson, and once my family left, the reality of "alone" would hit me. They left about 10:00 p.m. on Monday, and alone did hit. I recall shampooing carpets at 2:00 a.m.

Tuesday evening, the local newspaper came out online. One of the reporters had called me and we had gone over some things for the story on the accident. However, I was totally unprepared for what I saw when I searched online that evening. There on the front page was Terry's picture and the headlines "Bonita Welder Crushed in Construction Accident". The moaning, guttural screams came from deep within me, all too familiar by now; I felt them so deep; they came from my very soul! The reality. This just could not be happening.

Dick had told me he wanted to quit his job and try to run the business in Terry's absence. I was skeptical but after some time, he and I came to an agreement and we commenced.

About ten days had passed when the mortuary called that Terry's ashes were ready.

Dick said he would drive me in to pick them up.

I was still taking medication, not eating, and yet drinking, which had become worse, was in no shape to take on this task, but I did.

While at the mortuary, I was told the results of the autopsy. The cause of death was "contusion to the brain". Those words would stick with me for many months to come.

Terry's skull was crushed from the blow that knocked him to the concrete floor that day. The Police Report also stated Terry had "visible injuries to his head, face, and right arm, right side, right leg, and left foot. Both his right leg and right arm were broken." I remember as we left the mortuary, and I heard Dick say "are you ready?" I said "yes" and then he said, "I wasn't talking to you". He was asking Terry if he was ready to go home.

I only recall Dick getting me home and settling me into my chair. Terry's ashes were sitting on the hearth of our fireplace. The next thing I recall was waking up in the Emergency Room of the hospital with Dick, some friends and family around me.

Dick had left me with the ashes. I started drinking heavily. I don't recall it, but a friend had called me and while we talking to me she became concerned. Fearing that I had overdosed, she rushed to my home. I don't remember her arriving but when I opened the door, I collapsed. She called the ambulance and I was taken to the local hospital. I was told later that I had to be restrained, as I was too wild for them to handle. I was wild yes, I was wild with grief.

The next morning, I was released from the hospital with a diagnosis "Alcohol poisoning and grief".

That was Thursday Morning. The following Sunday was Father's Day, the day we had prepared to do the scattering of the ashes. My daughter said "Mom this is a sucky way to celebrate Father's Day". I told her that Father's Day would be awful one way or the other, so we may as well do what her dad would want for that day, to be scattered back across the valley. Friends were invited to join us. There were seventeen of us who made the 45-minute trek in four-wheel drive, up the steep mountain road to Grant Falls. Once we reached as far as we could go by vehicle, we had a few moments of prayer.

Terry always referred to the scripture of "dust to dust". Our great friend Mike read the following:

> *"Oh death where is your victory? Oh death where is your sting? The sting of death is sin, and the power of sin is the law; but thanks be to God who gives us the victory through our Lord Jesus Christ. Therefore my beloved brethren, be steadfast, immovable, always abounding in the work of the Lord, knowing your toil is not in vain in the Lord.*

For God who said "Light shall shine out of darkness" is the one who has shone in our hearts to give the light of the knowledge of the Glory of God in the face of Christ. But we have treasures in Earthly vessels, that the surpassing greatness of the power may be of God and not of ourselves; we are afflicted in every way, but not crushed, perplexed but not despairing; persecuted but not forsaken; struck down but not destroyed, always carrying about in the body, the dying of Jesus, that the life of Jesus may also be manifested in our body.

By the sweat of your face you shall eat bread till you return to the ground.....because from it you were taken: For you are dust, and to dust you shall return."

Me after we reached the hard climb to the top of Grant Creek Falls

Becca sang one of Terry's favorite hymns "Softly and Tenderly". It was a very emotional moment.

We began the hike up the mountain, which was about another 45 minutes or so. It was a beautiful but treacherous climb reaching the top. When we finally got there, I looked up to see the most beautiful waterfall!

The "guys" went on the climb to the top.

They helped our son Scott make his way.

Dick carried Terry's ashes in a backpack. Those of us at the bottom of the falls waited, sharing memories until we finally heard them at the top. After a gunfire salute, they were ready to scatter the ashes. We were sitting at the bottom of the falls. I didn't expect what was to come next. I had been watching up at the top of the falls when I heard my daughter say, "Mom, look!" I looked forward and saw my beloved's ashes, swirling and blending into the stream at the pool in front of me. As they blended, the color of the water changed. The green water became gray as the ashes became a part of the beautiful water in front of me. Once again came those all too familiar guttural groans from deep within me as I screamed and cried! Suddenly humor saved me. We had bottles of water. I asked someone to fill me a bottle from the swirling water in the falls. As he was leaning over to fill the bottle from the swirling water containing the ashes, he curiously asked, "Why do you want a bottle of this water?" I remember laughing as I said, "Terry always said he wanted to be put in a douche bag and run through one more time!"

We all laughed and the Terry Preas humor had, once again, saved me!

His ashes swirling in the water after they washed down the waterfall

High on That Mountain

You'd been there so many times before,
This time though was different.

The beauty of this place so serene...
A pool of life amongst trees and ferns.

You'd told us so many times in the past,
Though no one thought it would come.

33

Kittie Preas Koukalik

The jagged face of the stone worn smooth...
The powerful sounds of the water flowing down.

You wanted it to be this way so we came!
This time was your last time to make the journey.
The sounds of the birds singing their wonderful song...
Wind through the pines the air fresh and cool...
You imagined it this way friends and family together,
We were there with you climbing the slopes to the top.

From melted snow the water forms the sight we came to see.
Without having been there you'd not know its tranquility.

Your last wish that could be granted to you.

So proud we were to help you attain this ending goal...
With the path of the water we all watched you go!
For a final time you changed the world we all know.

You're gone from us now the water carried you away,
But forever in our hearts your precious memories will stay.

By Christopher Wacaster 6-18-2003

Grief is the price we pay for love
Elizabeth the 2nd

Dick was only 29 years old. While his intentions were good in the beginning, the stress of feeling he had Terry's shoes to fill was a heavy burden. The community was supportive but they also had high expectations that he would meet Terry's criteria. All the while, my emotional needs were crazy!

We agreed that he always would come to the house each morning for coffee so we could discuss the business plan for the day. That had always been Terry's routine with his workers. I needed something normal, as normal as it could be under the circumstances. Dick would come into the kitchen every morning for coffee and every evening before he left for the day. I hated that time, when reality set in. I was alone. It was these times when I drank. Though I have little or no recollection of those dark days, I know they were long, lonely and I wanted them to end.

I had to present "death certificates" to everyone it seemed! Though Terry and I had a will and things were in order; it took a hard four months to get the affairs settled.

I remember getting the letter from Social Security.

It read, "The marriage of Terry & Kittie Preas ended on May 28, 2003." How dare they!

I thought, "I will determine when this marriage is over!"

By now most of the many people who were at the house those first few days had gone back to their lives, and had left me with that enormous void in mine! I recall when I was really desperate; I would call some of those who had so freely spoken "if you need anything, call me". I would get an answering machine on which I leave a message. Most of them never called back. I slowly realized that people simply did not want to deal with their reality! This could really happen to them!

Within a few months I had lost 64 pounds. It was strange to find that the friends we had who were "couples" quickly ostracized me. It was apparent that the women considered me a threat to their marriage. I was suddenly considered "on the prowl and rated X", even though I had done nothing to indicate either of those things. I now saw that there was a clear "double standard" in place. If I had been a man left without a spouse, my friends would be trying to "set me up" and would be having me over for dinner. It became more apparent that I was a threat because I was a woman alone!

I had not only lost my best friend and spouse of 32 years, I had lost my identity, my place in the community and the thing that I would come to know later as "skin hunger". It consumed me.

A friend visited me one day. She had been suddenly widowed in her mid-forties. By now she was in her mid-sixties but I will always love her because she told me something that surprised me. She said that after her husband passed away "I thought my sexual appetite would never calm down!"

To hear this from this wonderful Christian woman made me feel that I was completely normal. While Terry and I had enjoyed a great sex life, suddenly it was gone and I was not only alone but I was extremely lonely. I had such "skin hunger"....

I craved physical contact!!

I recall mornings when I would wake and find my house in disarray, things out of place, furniture knocked over, and I would learn later that I had lost hours in my drunken stupor. These episodes later were diagnosed as "alcohol blackouts". Alcohol abuse had not been a problem for me when Terry was alive, however, upon his death; it was a very big problem. I wanted to numb the pain of reality. I didn't want to feel what I was forced to feel. It was during these blackouts that I did strange and irrational things.

Somehow I managed to get through the days. The activity at the welding shop, my work on the phone, typing up bills and contracts, and the job I used to have kept me busy. The nights were a different story. I grew to hate them. The weekends, which Terry and I always spent together, were another black hole.

We were either fishing or we would go to the casino and gamble. We loved that. Terry loved playing cards and was very good at it. The last Sunday he was alive, he told me he wanted to go to the casino in Tucson. I said, "Wouldn't you rather stay home and rest?" As usual he would reply with "I can rest when I'm dead". Little did we know that would come just three days later.

So we went. I am so glad I agreed to go. He won a big hand at the poker table and every slot machine he played, he won on. It was a great day! It was a common thing when he got to the casino to sign up for a poker game. When they got enough players, they would page him and I would hear "Paging Terry to the poker room."

About three weeks after his death, I was "running" on a weekend. I headed to that same casino, and on my way I stopped to see Bill, who had been one of Terry's right hand workers, and happened to be welding in the tank the day of his death. I asked Bill why Terry was in the tank that day. His reply was "Kittie, you know that was just Terry, always trying to help someone". My thought was one I would have for a long time "Why oh why couldn't you just stayed on the crane?"

Upon my arrival at the casino where we had spent our last good time just three weeks earlier, I sat down at a slot machine, put in a twenty-dollar bill and began to play nickels when I heard it. "Paging Terry to the poker room". I broke into sobs and cashed out my money and I promptly left the casino, cried all the way home. It was a long, long time before I returned.

There would be many incidents like that one. Terry had obtained a four-wheeler and loved riding it the short distance to the greenhouse. One day I saw a man riding one in that direction, wearing the denim shirt Terry always wore, a cap and for a split second I thought it was him. Once I heard a song on the radio that reduced me to sobs.

The lyrics were:

> *"Thought I saw you today*
> *You were standing in the sun then you turned away.*
> *And I knew it couldn't be but my heart believed.*
> *Oh it seems like there's something everyday*

How could you be so far away?
When you're still here…
When I need you you're not hard to find
You're still here
I can see you in my baby's eyes
And I laugh and cry
You're still here.
I had a dream last night
That you came to me on silver wings of light
I flew away with you in the painted sky
And I woke up wondering what was real
Is it what you see and touch or what you feel?
Cause you're still here
Oh you're everywhere we've ever been
You're still here
I heard you in a stranger's laugh
And I hung around to hear him laugh again
Just once again
Oh…
Thought I saw you today
you were standing in the sun then you turned away
Away …"

I would play that song again and again and cry.

There were many more that would come about. Alan Jackson "Remember When" was one.

Another Jackson song was "Monday Morning Church".

But Faith Hill's song was the one I seemed to torment myself with.

During those dark days, I rewrote my will. In the personal handwritten part, where I had left personal things to certain people, I wrote this personal note to my children.

"If I should die at my own hand, please don't be angry with me. It is just that I find it almost impossible to live with the pain of being here without your Dad!"

I got the chance in July of that year to go to New York City with my friend Joni and her girls.

A part of me didn't want to leave, as I had never made a trip that big without Terry.

But she and her daughters were going back to her class reunion so I agreed to go. It was a good trip. Among many things, we stood at the very site of "Ground Zero" where so many innocent people died just less than two years earlier. As we left the city that night to make the drive to Hudson to her sisters, I silently wept because I couldn't help but think how much Terry would have loved to see all of that. There would be so many things I would have to do without him.

You might wonder where our kids were in all this. Our daughter was in Tucson, attending the trade school she was going to when her dad died. She had promised him before the accident that she would finish. We spoke on the phone often but she didn't, couldn't come home. It was just too painful for her; she was daddy's girl and couldn't deal with it. So she threw herself into the schooling. Sadly, I wasn't much help to her.

I had all I could deal with just trying to deal with my own grief, and did not have to mental ability to take on hers as well. She didn't understand it and became resentful, a resentment that lingers to this very day.

Our son is mildly brain damaged from many years of massive seizures and had been in and out of special facilities for years. To make matters worse, he had also gotten into drugs, and had battled them long and hard. He won some and lost some. I am happy that he was doing well when his dad died and that he was clean and happy. However, after that he went over the edge. I desperately needed a strong supportive son, but I didn't have one. We all coped as best we could but we could not be supportive of each other, so we all suffered separately in our own ways.

In August of that year I made a trip to Texas and saw Terry's mom for the first time after his death. I took a video of the service, a lot of photos of the service, and some personal things for her and his little sister who lived with their Mom. Like his dad, Terry also played the harmonica, and so I took his treasured one and gave to his little sister.

There were many tears shed by all of us.

One night during that trip, as I slept at his brother's house in Ft. Worth, I had the first dream of Terry since his death. It was so real that waking and finding it was only a dream left me not only shaken, but also so extremely sad. In the dream, he was holding me and making love to me. It was not so much a sexual dream, as it was one of intimacy that only soul mates can experience. I could feel his soft kisses, his touch and his arms holding me. He was there! I will always believe it was not a

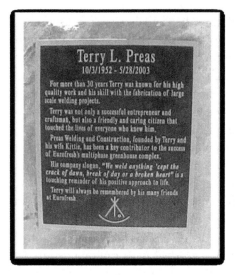

The bronze plaque Eurofresh erected in his memory

"dream" but rather a "visit".

In September of that year, there was scheduled a Memorial Roping to help raise money for us. It was called "The Terry Preas Memorial Roping". The only problem was, the facilitator failed to inform the people who entered that it was a benefit and consequently, they did not turn their prize money back, as was the custom in these benefit ropings, and so I only got shy of $400.00 from the roping. I also got a beautiful belt buckle that read "Terry Preas Memorial Roping 2003." Even though someone tried to steal it from me, I managed to recover it.

Eurofresh had told me they wanted to erect some kind of Memorial in remembrance of Terry. They decided on a very nice bronze plaque, which was erected at the gate where people enter the plant. Appropriately it was placed on a huge boulder, since Terry used to refer to his communing with God as "rock sitting".

It had his name, date of birth and death.

Then it reads "For more than 30 years Terry was known for his high quality work and with his skill with the fabrication of large scale welding projects.

Terry was not only a successful entrepreneur and craftsman, but also a friendly and caring citizen that touched the lives of everyone who knew him.

Preas Welding & Construction, founded by Terry and his wife Kittie, has been a key contributor to the success of Eurofresh's multiphase greenhouse complex.

His company slogan "We weld anything 'cept the break of day, the crack of dawn or a broken heart" is a touching reminder of his positive approach to life. Terry will always be remembered by his many friends at Eurofresh."

It also has his brand, an Indian Teepee at the end. It was a very beautiful and touching memorial to a great man who took much pride in Eurofresh and his work there.

The county road passing our home was named after what was once the "Hooker Ranch". It was named "Hooker Road". I despised that name enough when I had a husband but I knew I didn't want to live on it as a widow. Our home and shop was the only buildings on that road, the rest was just farmland. So I petitioned the County to change the name of the road to "Terry Preas Road". All of the landowners signed off in agreement and the county named the road after Terry. It blessed me so.

One of the large farming families wanted to purchase a Memorial Stone for Terry to be placed in our community graveyard. They told me to pick out what I wanted and they would pay for the stone and for having it set. I chose granite that was produced from Mt. Rushmore. It was a beautiful reddish color with flecks of gray. The family asked that our company logo be engraved at the bottom. They gave me the option of making it a double headstone and I chose to do that. His side has his name and date of birth and death, a drawing of the head of a man welding, which he used on his business cards. It had our last name in the middle of the stone, under that it says "In Remembrance". Under our last name are two hearts joined that has our date of marriage. Under the welding bust it says "Loving Husband, Devoted Dad, Faithful Friend". I chose these words because there were none that could have been more fitting. Down at the bottom is where the company logo is carved. It is a beautiful memorial stone.

I also adopted a mile of highway that was in Terry's favorite spot coming across the mountain. It says "In Loving Memory of Terry L. Preas."

Last but not least, I started a scholarship fund for our little rural school. Each year the "Terry Preas Memorial Award" goes to the graduating eighth grade student that has proven to be the biggest "over comer" to get where they are. I give a check and that student's name is placed on a beautiful cherry plaque.

I got through what would have been Terry's 51st birthday in October that year. I bought his favorite brand of whiskey, Gentleman Jack. I didn't even like whiskey. A friend and I drank the entire bottle that night.

I had made plans late that fall for the kids and myself to fly to Texas where we could spend Christmas with his family and mine. However as the dreaded holiday approached, it became more and more apparent that our son would not be making the trip with his sister and I. He was sadly doing his own thing. So we went without him. It was a very, very hard trip. We had always celebrated Christmas on Christmas Eve and I recall that evening, just sitting in a rocking chair, staring off into space, with the tears streaming down my cheeks uncontrollably, recalling all the of the Christmas Eve's we had shared in the 32 we had spent together. It brought me such gut wrenching sadness. I thought I would die and I wanted to. I didn't. Instead we turned the calendar for another year.

Running the Welding Business without Terry was more difficult than I ever imagined! I could handle the bookwork part of it but Dick knew nothing about how to figure and bid a job, or how to order steel. I am a good businesswoman therefore I was determined not be run over, or lose control of the business Terry had built, and died for!

Dick and I argued incessantly! It was a constant struggle for power and I was not giving that up. This business was mine. Dick was my employee and needed to conduct himself accordingly. Not only did he abuse use of the company truck and phone, but also abused his time while working.

I recall once going into the hair salon and saw him in the back with his feet propped up on the desk, visiting with the stylists. I reminded him discreetly that he was on the clock and needed to get back to work.

We had words about it later. This was just a small sampling of things we argued about.

Terry always stopped whatever he was doing when I went into the shop. Whether I was delivering a message, or needing to discuss something with him, or just to say hello, he always paused for however long it took. This was never the case with Dick.

He often seemed annoyed when I interrupted him with a phone message or had something to discuss with him. I recall one time when he saw me coming, he got mad and threw something across the shop! I was neither impressed nor entertained. I didn't feel it was appropriate to behave that way since I was his boss.

I fired Dick on more than one occasion, but then would realize how desperately I wanted and needed the business to continue. Though it was not making more than just enough money to support it, it gave me the emotional comfort I needed at that time. I knew that with the loss of the business, was total reality that Terry was dead, and I wasn't ready to accept that.

The State of Arizona required me to have a new "qualifying party" for the license, and to change the company name. Dick took the required test. I got the Bond and License and the business continued, this time under the new name of Preas Welding, LLC.

I was the owner.

We had enough work to keep him busy for the most part, but after fourteen months the constant bickering between us became more than I wanted to deal with. There was also a lack of accountability for some tools and supplies. And so it happened that in July 2004, I fired Dick one last time, sold him the truck and closed the business once and for all. It was painful but I was ready. Then I began the long and tedious task of liquidation. Terry had always told me that if anything ever happened to him, to go back to where we had bought the equipment and ask them what it was worth. I did so, they gave me a low and a high price and I hit a figure in between and set my price there. I had twelve welding machines, and countless other pieces of equipment. There were three trucks, two cranes, metal lathes, sheet metal brakes, and his precious Piranha Ironworker Machine.

Each time I opened the shop doors to show a piece of equipment, I was reminded that this was the last thing he ever wanted me to have to do. Yet I knew that he was watching over me and I hoped he was proud of me. I got what I asked for everything, in spite of folks who told me I wouldn't.

With each piece of equipment that left, a part of him left with it, and each time my heart broke, again and again. After twenty-two years, that chapter in our life was closed.

Yet for years to come I would have recurring dreams that Terry came back saying "how can I make a living when you sold all of my equipment?"

Unable are the loved to die--for love is immortality
Emily Dickenson

In November 2003, just months after Terry's death, I was turning fifty years old. I was not dreading the age, I was dreading facing fifty as a widow. I decided to have a birthday party. I invited many friends throughout our community; most of those who always came to Terry's fish fries. We fired up the smoker he had built, and smoked some meat. People brought side dishes and came to share my birthday with me. I was completely thrilled when two of my sisters, Karen and Wanda, told me they were coming from Fort Worth, Texas. We had a big crowd. I cried a lot, remembering with friends, and missing him, always missing him. That cold hard reality hit me often, Terry was gone, he was not returning. He had always taken care of me... we took care of each other, but now I had to take care of myself. The cavalry was not coming to save me. I had to save myself.

One night I was really depressed so I decided to do something I had never done in my life. I went into town to one of the local bars. I just sat at the bar and ordered a glass of wine. It wasn't long until a couple of men recognized me and walked over. One of the gentlemen had sold us a truck. He and I talked about Terry and how much we missed him, about his life, his death, and what he had meant to the locals in the valley.

We only talked. They never even sat down. After a while I left for home. The next few days the small town was full of rumors that I had been at the bar trying to pick up men.

Imagine my shock and the hurt to learn that a lady who has been in the bar had started the rumor. She also had been suddenly widowed at a young age. I thought it was strange that instead of coming over and talking with me, encouraging me, she started ugly rumors about me.

That was the end of my bar days in small town USA.

In early 2004, I began grief counseling. The counselor suggested that I write a letter to Terry, telling him how I was feeling about his death.

This is the letter I wrote, pouring my heart out to my darlin'.

"Dearest Terry,

You have been gone from me for 7 -1/2 long months now. I think that is about 5400 hours. I don't know how I have survived since that May 28 when you left me. Some days I still can't believe it. Then when nights like this one roll around, reality sets in. I can hear the sand hill cranes outside in the field. We always loved to listen to and watch them. The sound reminds me of you. Everything reminds me of you.

Darlin' HOW could you leave me? I know you really had no choice but couldn't you have just stayed in the crane that day and earned your money and let Marcos do his job? I always told you that your kind heart would be your demise.

I miss you more than I could ever tell you. I think some days I have done pretty well but other days I think my life is in shambles and you would be upset with me. Then I can recall how you always put your arms around me and said "It'll be okay" or "we'll make it...don't worry".

Well you aren't here and I don't think I can make it without you. I feel that you abandoned me when we had the best years of our lives ahead of us. Why did you have to go? You knew how badly I need you and how very much I love you!

You were my whole life and without you, I am like a ship lost at sea, no sail, and no direction, no will to stay afloat, just drifting among the waves, trying to stay on top, yet not really caring if I do or not.

There were SO many people at your memorial service, to honor you and the wonderful way in which you touched their lives. I hope you would have been happy with it, I know you would have. Then everyone came to carry out your wishes and spread your ashes in the waterfall. Scott made it to the top, with the guys help. You would have been so proud of everyone.... we chose to do it on Father's Day. Becca sang for you and Mike read scripture. You were and are still very much loved.

Scott has hit rock bottom again and I am glad you aren't here to see it, but wish you were here to help hold me up IN it. I don't know what to do. I can't help him when I can't help ME. I am a mess.

The County named our road "Terry Preas Rd" to honor you. The greenhouse put up a beautiful plaque in your memory, directly under the flags...and Bonita Grain bought you a memorial marker. They honored you in the Willcox paper this past week, referred to you as a "prominent citizen". Who would ever have thought that you would be called a "prominent citizen?"

David will be joining you soon. I know you know that and you will greet him with "hello my friend" as you did every morning when he came for coffee. I hope he remembers to give you my message..."I love you more".

Becca finishes school day after tomorrow. You would be so proud of her. She had a seizure the other night but is okay. She keeps pressing on just for you, so you will be proud of her.

Most of our friends have fallen by the wayside. I feel so very alone. Reach down and give me direction please. This whole valley misses you, but not nearly as much as I do, my love. For over 210 nights now I have climbed into our bed alone, wishing you were on your side, snoring, after you told me "goodnight darlin".... how I would love to hear that again! Why can't I feel your sweet presence?

Please reach down and help me to lose some of this anger I feel because you left me.

Even though I know you had no choice, I feel so abandoned and lost.

WHY did you have to go and WHY didn't you take me with you?

I love and miss you more than breath...

Love,
Your Kit"

Tears flowed as swiftly as the words I wrote.

David was one of Terry's closest friends and was heartbroken when Terry was killed.

David died eight months after Terry, of Melanoma.

He had come by for coffee with me in November, just two months before his death. He had not been by since Terry's accident. He spoke of how hard it was because it was a routine of his and Terry's. He told me tearfully how much he missed his talks with Terry. He said, as so many others had, that Terry didn't have the answers to life's problems but he always felt better by just talking to him.

Mike and I went to David's memorial service. At the given time for people to speak, I stood and read the following.

"Almost 8 months ago, we gathered here to memorialize and celebrate the Life of my husband and your friend, Terry Preas.

Today we come to do the same to his best friend, David Pigg.

Having known each other for over 25 years, and been as close as brothers for 23 of those years.... David was at our house for coffee most every morning. He would open the door as he yelled "knock knock", Terry would say "hello my friend" and as we three sat, the coffee flowed, the stories were told, and the friendship grew.

David and Terry were perfect examples that you don't have to have the same DNA to be family. They considered themselves brothers.

I recall the first time Terry invited David over for one of Terry's well loved fish fries.

David told Terry "I'll come, but I don't like catfish...can you cook me some crappie?"

Terry said yes he would, but we laughed because once David ate Terry's catfish...he was hooked. We always said it was a good thing David didn't like catfish or their wouldn't have been enough to go around. After that, he never missed a fish fry.

When David was offered the job on the Indian Reservation, Terry encouraged him to take it. I remember the last morning he was at our table for coffee before he left, they tried to hide their emotions, but each shed a tear or two.

Nonetheless, they spoke on the phone almost every day and when David would come back home, the morning coffees commenced.

It took David five months after Terry's death to return to our kitchen for coffee. He was very emotional as we visited and remembered the good times. David told me the thing he missed the most was not being able to "talk to Terry". He said, "I miss those talks more than anything, even five minutes on the phone with Terry was enough to get me going back in the right direction."

Two days after his visit with me David collapsed and the tumors were found.

Monday morning, January 19, 2004, at approximately 7:50 a.m. (just in time for morning coffee) Terry Preas heard a familiar voice say, "knock knock" at the door of Heaven. Terry hollered "Hello my friend!"

The coffee flowed, the stories were told, and the brothers were reunited..."

There was such irony in those two dying within eight months of each other. Death seemed all around me. In a year I had lost my favorite brother in law, my husband and his best friend. Death was smothering me. I needed to feel life, I needed to feel alive.

I knew God was with me but I could not feel Him. I tried to draw on my faith but it was difficult.

The God of the light is the same God of the darkness, in both good and bad, He is with us.

My head knew this but my heart couldn't find Him.

Sometimes you have to kiss a few frogs to find a prince

Shortly after my birthday party, I met a young man named Sean. I was 50. Sean was 24.

He didn't live in my small town, but in Tucson. Our friendship developed into a six-month relationship of sorts. I had needs and Sean was more than willing to meet them, safely, and it was a "no strings" deal. We met every weekend at his place. I would tell him later that he saved me from myself. He would tell me that I taught him much! Am I proud of my relationship with a young man more than half my age? No.

But I am not I ashamed of it either.

I survived being alone and we were two consenting adults. By today's standards, I would be called a "cougar".

But I defined myself as someone just trying to survive. Sean and I remain friends to this day and Tommy knows about our relationship.

In early 2004 I was introduced to a man I will call "Don". He was divorced, worked shift work at a plant about 40 minutes from me. He was just a few years younger than myself. When I met him, he didn't appear to be my type, but I was told he was a decent man and so when he asked me out, I accepted. We met locally, and he drove me to a nice place for dinner. This was my first actual "date "in 33 years.

Things had certainly changed since I was in the dating scene. It seemed all I could talk about was Terry. Don told me to stop apologizing but I tried to be more conscious of my words. We had a nice dinner;

visited, talked a lot and he drove me back to my pickup.

In the weeks to follow, we talked on the phone, and for the next months we met several more times for dinner. I had not yet invited him to my home. I was not comfortable with that and he respected my decision. He had never held my hand or even attempted to kiss me. He seemed to be a gentleman. However after a few months of this with Don, I began to worry. He had told me that I was "an attractive, intriguing woman". Yet he didn't appear to have any romantic interests. One night we were sitting outside a restaurant after dinner, just talking in

Kittie in 2004

his pickup. I finally said, "So are you ever going to kiss me?" He replied, "That would be nice". Although I was new to this, and it was so unlike me, I took the lead and moved over toward him and we kissed. It was nice. Then I moved back over to my side and that was that.

I thought it strange that he didn't give me his cell phone number, and never introduced me to any of his friends. He told me that he had only told two people about me, his best friend in California and a woman he had known since grade school, whom he would later betray me with. I didn't really know how it worked "these days" so I didn't question his decision to keep me a secret, but I always felt as though he was ashamed of me. I was a thin, and he said, a "beautiful woman". I had always been Terry's "arm candy". I didn't understand why I was a secret in this man's life.

When he told me he owned two Harley Davidson Motorcycles, I told him I would like a ride. I never got one.

Nonetheless, finally after the first anniversary of Terry's death, while on the phone with Don one night, I boldly told him I would like for this relationship to go farther. He asked me how far I wanted it to go and I just explained to him that I wanted it to be sexual.

I didn't know how else to tell him. It was not just sex that I wanted. I needed to feel arms around me, holding me in bed. I needed to hear a man snoring again.

I had continued my relationship with Sean up until this time; since it appeared Don and I were only acquaintances. But after the relationship with Don turned physical, I ended it with Sean.

One night Don came to my house for dinner, we ended up in my bedroom. Don was an "ok" lover. While holding me afterwards, he would gently kiss me on the side of my face, or kiss my hair. However he seemed to "check his heart" at the bedroom door. In looking back, I had such "skin hunger" that I allowed myself to be used a lot by this man!

When he apologized about his snoring, I told him I would never again complain about the sound of snoring, and I haven't.

On occasion I would go to his house and spend the night. When morning came, he seemed to always hurry me out, as though someone might show up and "find me there". After a few months of this, I began to feel used.

One night we had plans for dinner at my house but he didn't show up. I called him and got his voicemail. Later, he called back and said he had "forgotten". When he did arrive, I told him that this relationship was not working for me. That was our last "date".

After the incident at the bar in small town, I had sworn I would go out of town for fun.

I hated the weekends. They reminded me how alone I was, because Terry and I had always done something on the weekends. I started going to Tucson to a little bar called the "C Note Lounge". The owner's name was Terry. He had lost his wife to cancer just a few months after I lost my Terry. It was just a little dive bar but the band was great and I loved to dance. Over time "Terry 2" and I became great friends. I knew that while at his bar, I would be safe. I would get a room at a local motel and stayed at the dance until it closed. I loved to dance. When the men would hit on me, I had to keep saying, "I just came here to dance". My daughter and Terry's sons tried to get us together, however we felt that we would be better friends than lovers, so we kept it strictly friends. To this day we are still glad we made this decision. Still, we had many laughs together and cried some tears too. I went to that little bar and danced for months.

It was during these times that my 88 year old Mother would call from Texas to check on me. Getting my answering machine she would leave this message "Where oh where is my wild child?" She worried about me so.

Before I met Don, I had put my profile on two Internet Dating sites. I didn't want to see anyone locally then and certainly didn't after the bad experience with Don!

I did my research and decided that if I chose two sites that required a membership fee, it would weed out the ones who were not serious about finding a life mate. I chose Cupid.com and Match.com. Even though I kissed a few more frogs, that is where I would meet the man that would eventually be my second husband.

I had met some real winners online. The first one was the rancher from Vail. He was a nice guy but was so skinny; if we had been intimate his bones would have punctured me.

Then there was the veterinarian from Texas who was a real loser. Not only was he a terrible businessman but also didn't know what soap and water was.

There was the reporter from Phoenix who thought buying me dinner entitled him to a bedroom tumble in my motel room. He grew quite angry when he found out it didn't.

In addition, kissing him was like kissing a wall!

There was Don who "forgot" we had a date. Then the ex-hockey player who had migrated from Minnesota to Phoenix. He was a nice guy but something about him really annoyed me.

So far, the best thing to come from my "frog kissing" was the six months with the 24-year-old man!

I had ceased my relationship with Sean during my months of intimacy with Don.

However, once I kicked Don to the curb, I called Sean and asked him if he wanted to meet me in Tucson. He jumped at the chance. It was like two old friends getting together, only with "benefits".

I was on two online dating sites, but I never made any contacts. One of the sites, Match.com sent me random matches a couple of times weekly. One of the "matches" caught my attention because I loved his eyes, and loved his profile, so I "winked" at him. It was a couple of weeks before I heard anything back. Finally I received a "wink" back along with a "virtual rose". His username was "Goldwinger". I had no clue what this meant. Later I would learn he had a beautiful Honda Goldwing, which he couldn't wait to take me for a ride on.

My profile basically read:

"I am a young widow who is seeking a nice, sensitive man to spend some time with. I do not want remarriage at this time, maybe never. I like a gentleman; a country gentleman is even better. I was raised in the country, I live in the country. Anyone I spend time with needs to have a sense of self, sense of humor and be financially independent. Must be a romantic and not be afraid to express his feelings, without being haughty. Affectionate is a must. I must add, however, that I will not jump into bed on the first date so if you are looking for just a sex object, then move on. I love all that but am not the type to just have sex with strangers and I do not consider a few emails, phone calls and dinner, knowing a man well enough to give myself to him. Old fashioned? You bet and proud of it. That does NOT mean that I cannot be good in the sack, (want a note?) but just that I would like to be courted first. I find that what I miss the most since my husband's death is ROMANCE! My favorite movie of late is "Something's Gotta Give". I also believe I am a "woman to love" which scared off my first relationship since being widowed. By his own admission, he traded "Fillet Mignon" for "Green Bologna". His loss could be your gain…

I am independent and though I am still in grief, I am trying to continue with my life…wanna take my hand and walk me through?"

"Goldwingers" profile was lengthy but what caught my eye were the following words:

"I am described as the one that can be counted on… always. I am happiest when I can make another smile. I am at peace when I take the time to "smell the roses". I am a "hopeful romantic" and have read, "Men are from Mars, Women are from Venus".

A lady (in all sense of the word) does not need a man but does want a man in her life. She can stand on her own two feet but is not afraid to take a helping hand (or to hold hands in public). She can hold her own in conversation and looks good in a tee shirt and jeans or a formal gown."

When I finally heard back from him, he just told me he worked for Pima County. I thought "Gosh I hope he isn't a trash man or something". While that was an honorable job, it wasn't what I had in mind for a partner.

We emailed back and forth through the Match.com's secure system for a few days, finally felt secure enough to exchange personal emails. Eventually we exchanged phone numbers and talked on the phone. We agreed to meet halfway for each of us on Sunday, December 12, 2004, for dinner. I asked him what he drove; he told me and also told me what his personalized license plate was. I gave him my vehicle information, including the personalized plate information. He said "I have seen that plate somewhere. I never thought I would get to meet the beautiful lady driving it". I was skeptical at the time, however much later I believed him when I found out he was in Law Enforcement and he really does observe license plates.

Ironically the restaurant we met at was also the one Don had taken me to on our first date. I was a size twelve then, dressed in a pretty blue sweater, jeans, boots and wore my black fringe, western suede jacket that I wore most everywhere. I had red hair.

I drove up to the restaurant at the proper time and his truck was there, backed in, as though he thought he might want to make a rapid escape! Upon my arrival and locating him in the small place, he quickly stood to greet me; I shook his hand and then promptly excused myself to use the ladies room. When I came back to the table, he stood again. I thought "what a gentleman!" We ate, and visited, and upon completion of our meal, we decided the restaurant needed our table, so I asked him if it would be okay to sit in his truck and talk. We did so, and that talk lasted over two hours. He didn't try to hide the fact that he was quite smitten by me, and the fact that I did indeed look like my photo! At one point he asked me what he had to do in order to "get on my list". He even placed his fingers inside his jaw and did a crude but cute "Reel me in".

While Tommy aka "Goldwinger" was smitten with me, I must admit I did not feel the same. He was very much a gentleman. But there was just something about him that bugged me. I didn't feel there was any attraction at all. I had a long drive ahead of me, as did he and he had to work the next day, so we parted ways, not before I explained to him that I was leaving on Thursday, for Texas, to surprise my Mom for her 88th birthday.

Tommy called me before I got home, to make sure I had made it home safely. He also told me he had no problems dealing with the memories I had with my late husband, and would consider it an honor to help me through the remaining grief.

Precious memories...how they linger...how they ever flood my soul

Often it was difficult for Terry to get to the store for a card, and in these times he would leave me a note on the cabinet or write me a letter. These meant more to me than any store bought card could have ever meant. I would like to share some here in no particular order.

He had purchased a blank book for the purpose of writing our favorite recipes. I found this one after his death.

To Kit

Recipe for a good marriage:

1 young lady in your eyes to take your breath away.
1 young man whose girl makes his heart beat a little faster.
2 hearts that race at the touch of hands together

Cook at medium boil from first kiss.
Time set for wedding day
1 dash of happiness
31 years of heated passion

He never got to complete this recipe.
After a very lean few months due to his back injury, this was his last

Valentine's Day note:
A heart drawn on a piece of paper with a note left at the coffeepot that morning.

"Too broke for a card or candy, will try to do better next year.

Terry"

Note left for 30th Wedding Anniversary

"Dear Kit,

I can't believe it's been 30 years this day. It seems like only yesterday two kids started out on life's road together. You have been a great traveling partner. I can't see going anywhere without you.

May we have another 30 years together. I want to say thanks and that I love you."

He signed it with his signature Indian Tee Pee

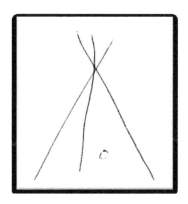

**The Indian Tee Pee he
used to sign his notes to me**

Left on the kitchen cabinet Valentine's Day 2002

"Kit,

It's Valentine's day 2002. You have been my sweetheart for some time now. (31 years).

57

I know you have had some disappointments, but I want to say thank you for all you have done.

The Love I have in my heart is so great, but it doesn't stop there. Respect, honor, admiration, friendship, companionship, and a thousand more things I cannot express.

I hope you have a happy V-Day.

Love,"
(Tee pee drawing)

And another for our 28th anniversary

"Kit

Today we begin our 29th year together. "Who'd a thunk it"? I love you so!!! I'm thankful

for our times together. May we sit on our porch 28 more.

I Love you"
(Tee Pee drawing)

November 2002 - My last birthday with him.

Happy Birthday

"Dear Kit,

When we were just kids, I knew I'd found the love of my life. I can remember the first time you really looked into my eyes. The things I saw changed my life. Every time I hold you in my arms and look into your eyes, I can still see why I wanted to share my life with you.

I know that the storms of life took its toll on both of us. Through all the struggle of hard work, you made it worth it to me.

There were very difficult times and I know that I bailed.

You were the strongest yet most fragile person that I have ever known. You saw the world in black and white, staunch in your belief. I, on the other hand went through my young life with a driven vision of success...

After 31 years I'd like to sum it all up:

First you have become my best friend.
Second you're my lighthouse in a world of darkness.
Third is the love we share
Fourth, as a lover, it is truly a gift from God.

Time will not permit me to list all the things that are in my heart. To do so, would take the remainder of my life.

With all the love in my heart,
Terry"

(He didn't know the remainder of his life would be so short)

About 2000, Valentine's Day.

"To My Valentine Kittie

Kit, you have been my Valentine for a while. I don't have words to tell you what's in my heart. All the years, heartache and tears. Through, what seems like forever in one way seems like yesterday in others. You will be my Valentine for eternity.

May we have fifty more years to be mates on this earth.

With the love of eternity.
Terry"
(Tee Pee drawing)

I don't know what year the following was written. It was two small tear out pages folded. On the front he wrote "Poor Boys Mother's Day

Card". Inside he had written:

> *"Kit,*
>
> *I didn't get you anything for Mother's Day but I want you to know that I think you are a great Mom who has had more to deal with than most, but still did a remarkable job. You have been the best 'life's mate anyone could have ever dreamed of I think sometime I can't go on with the way things are going, but you seem to get a grip when I can't, so I think I'll keep you! I love you more than you know.*
>
> (Tee Pee drawing)
>
> *P.S. Happy Mother's Day"*

Terry was also known for what we called "Terryisms".
Here are just a few I can recall.
One of the earliest that Terry would never live down was during the time we were dating. He wanted more from me than I was taught to give unless I was married and his line was "In God's eyes we are already married".
The ones from later in his life were regarding hunting and fishing. "They call it 'hunting, otherwise it would be called 'getting' if it was easy."
"A bad day fishing beats a good day working anytime."
When folks at the cleaning station of the lake saw all his big fish, they would say "where did you catch those fish?" Terry was serious as could be as he stuck his finger in the corner of his mouth and replied "right here".
When Terry and I would tease each other, I would say to him "you better behave or I will cut you off". He would smile and jokingly say "You can't cut me off; you don't know where I'm getting it".
Another one he had regarding me was after someone had made me angry. He would just shake his head and say "You pissed her off, now you deal with her".
He would always tell our kids to "bow their heads and bend their knees".
Terry was a praying man.

He would also tell them "Remember who you are".

Our daughter married a man who had one arm covered with tattoos. Now these things were a big no-no to Terry. One evening we were all sitting on the patio and Terry asked Ray why he would ever get tattoos. Ray replied "oh I was about 17 and got drunk and some friends talked me into it." Terry's reply was a record maker as he said "son, I have been drunker than a waltzing piss ant and I never got any tattoos". Ray still laughs about that one.

Regarding work, he always said "man made it, man can fix it".

Someone would ask him "how are you" His reply was one of these:

"If I was any better I would have to call out my own name during sex!"

Or "Busier than a one armed paper hanger".

Or "busier than a one legged man at an ass kicking contest"

Or "Up to my ass in alligators and somebody drained the swamp"

Old friends and I still laugh at those and they bring smiles to our faces.

Terry was a man who despised "Religion" but was very spiritual. He felt very attune with God while out in the woods, or the lake and he always believed in, and looked for signs from God. That is why there were certain things that happened after his death that I knew were signs for me, from Terry, letting me know that he was still with me.

Like the day after the service when the pop thunder storm 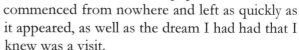 commenced from nowhere and left as quickly as it appeared, as well as the dream I had had that I knew was a visit.

We both loved roses and had many rose bushes in our yard. One rose bush in particular was a WHITE one that is right under the kitchen window. It was not uncommon for me to see him walk past the window after a long day's work, stop at the rose bush and look to find the perfect rose, cut it off with his pocket knife and bring it in to me. I always acted surprised! About three months after his death, on this WHITE rose bush, two pink roses appeared. I knew they were from him to me. It was a sign to me that he was still with me. I would just walk by them, stop and smell and say "I love you too darlin'." They continued every season for three years and each new season, I would wait with anticipation to see if they came back. He was still with me.

One morning less than a year after his death, I was in our bed and was soundly asleep.

I could hear Terry in the kitchen, doing all the things that he did every morning. I recognized the actions by sound. I could hear his bending over to lace up his work boots, putting his coffee cup into the sink, and then I felt him sit down on the side on the bed. He sat ever so gently on my side, so as not to wake me. Terry always loved to watch me sleep. Though I was dreaming, it was so real and I knew this was also one of those rare "visits". I treasured them so much.

Another incident that I would say was very spiritual happened two year later.

I had surgery June 28, 2005. The morning of what would have been our 34th wedding anniversary, I painfully got out of bed to go to use the bathroom. It was just a few days since my surgery and I could hardly move. As clear as could be I heard Terry's soft voice say "Darlin', are you okay?" It was almost an audible voice. It brought me great comfort.

This was also written in tribute to Terry.

Gathering Light---A Pilgrimage

With a yearning for adventure in his early life-----a change he chose,
Causing a move from Texas to Arizona…
farming country where most anything grows.

Nestled in the Sulpher Springs Valley learning lots about local trades,
Enjoying many tests along the way… with the end product proudly displayed.

Learning the art of sheet metal intrigued him to master other mediums as well,
Then being inquisitive enough to subdue challenges presented by all his clientele.

People attracted his interests which meant visiting was a must,
While picking their brains he would remember nearly all the details discussed.

He knew and admired that God created many great works to view,
Which attracted him and gave lasting desires to be part of his crew.

Liking the out-of-doors, animals, hunting and fishing gave him reason to admire,
The beautiful sun, moon and star-decked heaven as he reminisced around the camp fire.

Serious about life, friendships and family,
yet known to be a bit of a joker, even on his night out with the guys playing a low stakes game of poker.

Bestowed with a positive approach toward all things concerned was a trait,
He applied that to his work ethics as well as he cherished family, especially his mate.

When presented with a project to construct he thought, planned and built it neat,
so roundabout can be found much of this creative handiwork he did complete.

Basically, a true craftsman with materials, people, pleasures and time were instilled from the start,
and a company motto of "we weld anything 'cept the crack of dawn, break of day or a broken heart."

This caring and hard working citizen truly enjoyed his work while finding opportunities for fun,
meaning he knew not that he had limited time to finish the many things left undone.

Treating people fairly was evident in his dealings with mankind while being well mannered and polite,
showing his life among us should be an inspiration as was his journey of gathering light.

Delivered from darkness on October 3, 1952, then on May 28, 2003 he entered the realm of God's peace,
In summation, these mindful facts amply fit the life and the beautiful person--

--Terry L. Preas.

-written with admiration and love
by Robert (Bob) L. Haupert
Farmington NM.
July 15, 2004

If you don't go after what you want, you'll never have it

Goldwinger must have believed this as he continued to pursue me. We had met for the first time on Sunday December 12, and on the next evening he phoned me and said "I need a Kittie fix before you leave for Texas". He asked if I could meet him again the following evening and we could drive to Sierra Vista and see a movie. I agreed.

When I arrived to meet him, he was already there with a big grin on his face and smelling really well! We talked and visited on our journey and I played the CD of my daughter singing. I shared with him about the upcoming flight to Texas and how I knew I was really alone when I returned at the airport and there was no one to meet me. He asked several question about my flight but I never thought anything of it and gave very vague information.

When we went into the movie theater there was no one yet there and I teased him about buying out the entire theater. During the movie I decided I would let him hold my hand. I was ready but being a big popcorn fan, he kept his hand in a bucket of popcorn! I had about lost my nerve when he finally finished, and I told him my hand was cold. He eagerly covered my hand in both of his. It felt at home there. After the movie was over we went to dinner and when he dropped me off, I had a strange urge to let him kiss me but decided it was too soon.

(I later learned he had the same urge and thought) I made my trip to Texas and I called him once while I was there. He was very pleased.

When I left for my flight home, I had that awful feeling once again of arriving at the airport and having no one to meet me, reality stinks.

I got off the plane and walked down the tarmac, staring down at my feet, thinking about having to take a shuttle and claim my vehicle. All of a sudden my eyes looked up as I saw this person holding a Kilroy sign with my name on it. It was up above his face but when I stopped, it slid down and there he stood...Tommy aka Goldwinger!!! He had a purple, gold trimmed enamel rose for me and welcomed me home, so that I would realize I wasn't alone. He had jumped through hoops to get my flight information. I thought "You know, if a guy listens this much and goes to this much trouble to make my day, he at least deserves a chance!"

We went for a glass of tea; he had to get back to work. I must admit I was impressed.

He was sweeping me off my feet and I thought to myself "just keep sweeping!"

I had told him how much I dreaded Christmas Eve, as that was when we had always had Christmas. He asked me how long since I had been to Winterhaven, the Festival of Lights. I didn't know what he was talking about, as I had never been. He told me what it was and I told him I would love to go. We made plans and I told him I would bring homemade soup to his home which we would have after the ride through the lights.

With the holidays approaching, I was thirsting for a future but was so hung up in grief and the past. I wrote the following letter to Terry, in hopes of relieving some of my pain.

Christmas 2004

"My Darlin' Terry,

This is the second horrible Christmas without you. It's been so many years since that wonderful Christmas Day 1970, that you and I met for the first time. You went home and told you Mom you had met the girl you were going to marry. I always teased you about that. Though I was just hardly 17 and you 18, we fell so hard for each other and few were shocked when we got married July 1971. Just kids, but we knew we loved each other with a love that eventually proved to beat the test of time! Sick kids, times when you were ill, no matter what, we always loved each other and stuck it out. Every marriage has hard times and we had more than our share, but our love kept us going.

I was always so fearful of life, lost without you by my side telling me it would be okay.

You had a way of "putting hope in hopeless" and in "making crazy, sane." I never felt like a whole person without you by my side. We talked about growing old together and I remember one night I lay in your arms and you said "I hope we die like this, in each other's arms".

But God and fate had other plans. May 28, 2003, my life ended with yours. I watched you scream in pain and death that day and all I could say was "I'm here". For months I agonized over whether you knew I was there as you took your last breath, but one day I realized YOU WAITED FOR ME!

You knew I was coming and though I feel your spirit had already left your body, you waited. (You always put me first).

I find such irony in the fact that we painfully watched our kids have seizure after seizure for so many years, seeing them finally steal our son from us, and yet God had such a sick sense of humor that a grand mall seizure was the last thing I saw from you as you took your last breath.

As I have read in a grief book "I hated God that day. I fired God that day. How could He decide your wonderful life on this earth was over without even consulting me? Not a loving God!"

As I sit here now with tears streaming, I have a myriad of emotions. I am trying so hard to make you as proud of me in death as I did in life. I would have joined you already if not for fear of disappointing you.

You told me 'Kit, if anything happens to me and you stop living, I will be so disappointed in you'.

And so I trudge on, trying painfully to live each day without my Terry. Who am I without you? I am a rudderless ship, drifting, trying to find my way alone for the first time in my life.

This year I put up a small Christmas tree. I did your job of putting on the lights. I put red bows on it and your Christmas Ornament "Merry Christmas from Heaven".

I cannot yet take out "our tree", with its years and years of memories and ornaments.
I am alone.

Becca had a seizure yesterday and I don't want her driving. Scott is back in the hospital. We are all such a mess.

When, oh when, will this ache for you stop? I miss you darlin', more than breath!

Your Kit.......forever changed"

I can't say it brought me much relief. I kept putting one foot in front of the other, in hopes of finding that special someone who would love me for what Terry had loved me for, and not hurt or use me.

There is no such thing as too much hug
Winnie the Pooh

Tommy sent me directions to his home. I was expecting a meager bachelor pad. I arrived with my soup to a beautiful, less than two year old home, clean and beautifully decorated. Tommy was waiting for me outside, complete with Santa Hat. I thought him to be such a "goober" but I had to smile at his enthusiasm! Inside he had soft Christmas music playing and was burning a wonderful Christmas candle. I was impressed!

Our ride through the Festival of Lights was wonderful, as he sat with a blanket over us for warmth. When we got off the mule wagon, he opened the door to my side of his pickup to let me in. While he was going around to his side, I slid over to the middle. His smile upon opening the door was worth a million and with PERFECT timing he leaned over and kissed me! Perfect timing indeed!

We headed back to his house and had my wonderful homemade soup. We watched Christmas movies in front of the fireplace with a blanket over our feet and legs. He was the perfect gentleman. When it was time to go to bed, he asked me if I wanted to sleep in the guest room or share a bed with him, assuring me that if I chose the latter, he would be a perfect gentleman. I chose, for some reason, to share his bed. Perhaps it was to just feel someone next to me, arms around me, but for whatever reason, this was my choice. We both slept in flannel pajamas. He was the epitome of a gentleman and held me close all night. He had passed the test.

I left the next afternoon to have Christmas with my kids, he with some friends. I knew when I got back to his house that I would be sharing his bed again that Christmas night, only this time without the flannel pajamas... It just felt right.

Like the night before, we snuggled on the leather love seat and watched Christmas movies. The fireplace was going and we had a blanket spread over us. Every now and then our feet would "snuggle". I felt as though I had known the "gentle" man forever. I stayed a couple more days and it felt so right. I loved cooking in the big kitchen, sleeping in the big bed that was so tall I had to use a little step stool. The feel of his arms around me as we slept the warmth of his body as it curved against mine was pure Heaven!

In thinking about my past relationship, I could only think "Don who?"

When I had to return home, I felt lost, as did he. He would email me and tell me he couldn't sleep without me in the bed. This went on for about a month. I went back and forth to his place. We had plans for him to visit my home for the first time in late January. I was excited but nervous. My little home that love built was so small compared to his. What if he didn't like the fact that I lived way out in the country?

He arrived one night after work; it was dark when he finally rang the back door bell. I was thrilled to open the door and see him standing there, still in his uniform, with bag in hand. After a hug and kiss, he asked me to show him around. I did so, and was proud to show him all the things in the house that Terry had built. I had shared a lot with him about my late husband. He was never jealous, and was always respectful and even emotional. We shared my bed that night. He belonged there. The next day with the sun shining, I showed him around at the big shop that was Preas Welding & Construction. I told him about where this machine set or that one. I had already told him what all I had sold, but pointed out that there was still much to be done, and it was to the point of my needing help. Guess who stepped up to the job?

I needn't have worried; he loved my home, the shop and the beautiful valley. When Sunday evening came, we both knew he would have to start heading for home. We had put it off as long as we could. I climbed up and sat in his lap on the sofa and put my arms around his neck. I kissed him and said tearfully "Don't go". He looked up at me, those gentle eyes that had first attracted me to him were full of tears as he said "don't do this, I'll be back". I said "that's what Terry said too and he didn't come back". But we both knew he had to go. With his absence, the house seemed once again, very empty and lonely. But I had enjoyed so much, sharing my world with him.

Tommy and me at his USAF Retirement

I think one of the hardest things in grief work is giving us permission to go on and live, to realize that our loved one would want us to do so. I put a post it note on my bathroom mirror that read "Kit, if something happens to me and you stop living, I will be so disappointed. --- Terry." He had told me that and I needed to remind myself that life could go on for me, if I let it.

It was a few months into the romance with Tommy that I showed up at his home right before he got off work.

When he got home, he found me in his big garden tub, with lots of bubbles and two glasses of wine. As he joined me in the tub, I looked at him with tears in my eyes and I said "I came to tell you that I think I am falling in love with you". He smiled, touched my face with his hand and said "I am already there, why are you crying?" I replied "because Terry is still in my heart". He said "I would be honored to share it with him".

In March 2005, CMSgt Thomas Koukalik retired after 34 years with the USAF. I was proud to stand by his side.

In June he had a business trip to Palm Desert, California. He asked me to join him and I was all too happy to do so. We made the trip together, and stayed at the beautiful resort! While he was doing his classes, I made a tour with the "wives" through Palm Springs. It was a good trip.

In spite of my new found love, the grief didn't end. In fact, at times it may have made it worse. We have such issues with "moving on" and society doesn't help. Just when we think we can look past and get on with our lives, someone pops off and says something they think is "helpful". I wrestled with my old life and my new one.

The goal of my recovery should be to learn to live with my loss and to adjust to my new life. I will never forget; recovery from my loss will be like a scar that remains after a surgery. It makes sense that certain circumstances or memories will make the scar ache or throb. It reminds me of my loss and I will have to do something to tolerate the pain until it passes.

Grief will bring many changes. I lost my identity. I so wanted my grief journey to be a stepping stone to pass on to others who were hurting and feeling hopeless!

While I had no control or choice over Terry's dying, I did know that I wanted to love and be loved again. It involves a risk, as does anything worth having.

My recovery from the intense grief did not mean that I would forget Terry or the life we had together. I believe instead, that when one loved as I did, I will forever mourn to some degree. And so, I pressed on.

Feb. 6, 2005 I wrote:

"Once upon a time, in a land far away from the city of Willcox, in a little valley called Bonita, there lived two people. This man and woman were so much in love that he referred to her as his "Queen" and she referred to him as her "King". The King and Queen married young but their love and commitment to each other was so strong that the marriage weathered the birth and rearing of two chronically ill kids, their own illnesses, deaths of friends and family members and much more. Still their love for each other remained strong and solid. They owned and operated a business that serviced a vast area and the King worked very, very hard while his Queen helped him and stood by his side through whatever the forces of evil threw their way. They were very blessed and they knew it.

One day, May 28, 2003, their little world ended when the King was in a terrible accident and the Queen was informed that her King was dead! The Queen and her children wept and wondered how their lives would ever be the same without their King, who was a beloved husband, friend and dad. The Queen's heart was so broken that the castle began to crumble around her and she wished she could join her King in eternity (never never land) but her wishes were not granted. She struggled alone, as friends vanished like they were afraid her sadness and her loss of her beloved King was contagious. She wept alone in her crumbling castle for many, many months as she struggled to survive her life without her beloved King.

She thought that she would surely die from her broken heart and she really didn't care. Her main purpose in life was to find the courage (heart) to survive as to not dishonor her beloved King. He had once told her that if anything happened to him and she stopped living, he would be very disappointed in her. The Queen realized there were many ways in which to stop living. There was the way of ceasing to breathe, and there was also a way of ceasing to savor life and live it to its fullest, as her King had always done.

She bewailed and she mourned and she felt so very lost. Her very life was so intertwined with the life of her beloved King that she knew not who she was without him.

The DGI's (People who DON'T GET IT) judged her every move. She tried to overlook their judgments as she realized their doing so was mostly out of ignorance because they still had their Kings.

One day she met a handsome prince and her heart came to life again and she began to realize that maybe she COULD find love again and that maybe life COULD go on. A DGI said that this must mean that she was "over" the terrible loss of her beloved King. She was outraged and hurt that someone could be so cruel as to indicate that anyone would ever replace her King in her heart.

She pondered on this, searched her soul and realized that she had done exactly what her King had wished for her. She had found the courage (heart) to live again, not only to stay alive but to actually live again. She never stopped thinking that her King would walk past the window of the castle after a long days work, whistling, and walk into the room with a hug and a kiss for his Queen. But in her heart she knew that this would never, ever happen again as her beloved King was truly gone......dead...and would never again return to the castle they built together.

If they had lost a child and gone on to have another, would people think that meant they had gotten over the loss of the dead child? Not at all. Yet people

Terry and me in 1999

perceive being a widow in a different light.
The only people the Queen has to answer to is
her God, her beloved, departed King and herself
and she believes, yes she knows that all three are
smiling on her, for once again, even through the
tears of grief, her heart has found a happy place
and at least some peace has swept over her soul.

The End....

written by Kittie Preas
Goodnight Darlin'
I love you more"

Writing was what my grief counselor encouraged me to do, and so I wrote all the things that were deep in my soul and all the things I wished I could say to Terry!

In the summer of 2005, I found this on the internet and I modified it and wrote it to Terry. The author gave me permission to use it.

To Terry

Another Day

For months I dreaded the sunsets and their memories of more pleasant ones
shared together, because they only marked the passing of another day without
you.

And then I embraced the sunsets and their pain claiming they marked the
survival of another day without you but found myself merely waiting for grief
and time to end somehow.

Now as I sit beneath a cloudless sky watching the long shadows of the
mountains trace across the land at sunset

I smile, somewhat feebly, as memories of more pleasant ones shared together,
mark another day passing in my life, instead of hours spent without you, and
want more time to become myself again, to collect this shattered mess into

something more than sorrow.

Sorry my love, but you were not ALL that I WAS (just as you used to tell me!).

Neither one of us arrived empty handed when we met, and we both grew and gained before we had to part.

Many people contributed to the things inside me.

It's just that death casts such poignancy into memories that perspective is lost for so long a time.

And speaking to you without getting lost in the sadness is still difficult.

Your accident and death showed me that the things I've valued most came from what you taught me,

And at one point, you helped a shy and insecure young girl to care about more than herself as she learned to understand what "to love and to cherish" means.

And in its practice, love brought us more than we had before and made us more than we were by ourselves, alone.

So if you've eyes among those stars emerging from the darkening sky, you'll see I carry parts of you forward with me.

I can't live out what might have been the rest of your life for you, but as I live out the rest of my life for me.

Your love, your life, and your spirit are here.

They are things I treasure and hold dear, and I no longer have fear of their fading.

Your spirit was bright before it met mine and doesn't require me as its keeper.

I can only pass on what comes from the best of both of us.
Human nature being what it is, you'll have to pardon the times I take more
credit for myself than is due, but when I give of myself and find joy in this life
I know in large part, the credit should go to you!

The things I've been and the things I miss are most certainly part of what I've
now become. And although, after 3 years, there is still a bit of emptiness or
hollowness to it all, it is again, finally, somehow okay to be here and to take
joy in just living.

From Kit
Goodnight darlin'......I love you more..."

Written originally by Michael Goshorn... modified by Kittie Preas... used
with permission

Grandchildren are God's reward for not killing your kids

In December 2005, my daughter made me a grandmother for the first time. Trinity Lynn, middle name after Terry, entered this world with me at one side of her mother's bed, urging her to "push". Weighing over 8 pounds, she had a host of medical issues.

Trinity was born with a complete cleft palate, though her lip was normal. She had extreme respiratory distress after her birth and for these reasons was placed in the NICU, where she spent four weeks. I visited every day. After about two weeks, the doctor did an MRI on Trinity and saw evidence that she had suffered a stroke while in her mother's womb. Estimation was that this happened at about seven months gestation. Because of this, she had soft spots on the frontal lobe of her brain and was given the diagnosis of "cystic encephalomalacia".

God and I had been at a "standoff" for some time, and Terry's death didn't help matters any. One day while Trinity was in the NICU, I stayed with her while her mom went for a doctor's appointment. When Trinity was finally resting, I made my way to the all too familiar hospital cafeteria to get some lunch. On my way I passed the beautiful hospital chapel. I was very familiar with this chapel, as I had spent forty days at this same hospital in 1989 when our son had suffered a terrible accident. I had made a few visits to the chapel. This day I felt drawn in there. I was alone and so I took a seat at the front, facing the strikingly beautiful stained glass windows.

As I sat there I began to cry. the tears flowed as I talked to God. I recall saying "okay God, you got me here. You took my normal son, and then you took my husband and now you have taken my granddaughters health. She was supposed to have been one who brought healing to this family. I am angry God, and I am heartbroken. But I give her back to you, because you gave her to us. There is nothing else I can do."

**Me holding Trinity
after her Christening**

I left there that day feeling like a heavy burden had been lifted from my body.

With the birth of Trinity, new stages of grief hit both me and her mom.

We so wished that Terry could have been here with us to share in this blessing.

He would have been such a wonderful grandpa and he would have loved her so!

Having her here and without him introduced a roller coaster of emotions that I thought had gone from me.

Making a new life with another man after spending 32 years with the same man can have its unique set of problems. While it was no fault of Tommy's, I knew that Terry and I had been so close that he knew me better than I knew myself. Emotionally he always knew just what to say. He knew when I was worried, how to give me encouragement, and could do so even if he didn't have a clue how he was going to work things out. He would often hug me and say "It'll be okay". Then he would try and figure out how to make it okay. Terry had a calming effect on not only me but on his friends. He also knew my body and he knew how to meet my needs. He "played my body like a fine guitar". One would expect this would be the case after so many years together. As I said, this means no disrespect to Tommy. Terry and I found ourselves finishing each others' sentences. We would both bring up the same subject at the same time. It was uncanny! We would see an old couple wobbling and holding hands and he would take my hand and say "Mama that will be us in a few years".

Terry and I also were able to deal with the issues regarding our son together. It is far easier when the kid belongs to the both of us. Tommy tried, but he had no children and didn't have parenting skills. He was a supportive as he could be, but he really couldn't do much from his position. All of this brought on issues for Tommy and I that we had to work through. During the time that I was going to grief counseling, I learned that it is never just one thing that puts us over the edge. This was the case with me, when approaching the third anniversary of the accident, I had a number of issues I was trying to deal with and I buckled. For the first time, Tommy and I had words and I packed a bag and left. I took a big bottle of wine and checked into a motel. However, I checked into the one where I had told him I used to stay during my weekends of dancing at the C Note Lounge.

I don't recall much of that night. I was told I called my son, who then called my daughter and they decided that they should encourage Tommy to try and find me. He did so and knew where to look because that is where I used to stay. I had told the manager of the motel that I didn't want to be bothered. When Tommy showed up at the desk inquiring about me, he was told I didn't want phone calls or visitors. Tommy said he spoke to me on the phone and I told him he could come up to my room and talk but when he got there I wouldn't open the door. He finally had to discreetly call some fellow officers who were on duty and have them make the manager let them in.

I was told that I finally opened the door and spoke to a woman Sergeant, and she saw the empty bottle of wine and observed my state of mind and called an ambulance. By then my daughter was there and I was, once again, transported to the hospital, and have no memory of it as I was in a blackout. Tommy told me later that I kept calling his name and crying while I was in the Emergency Room. He sat with me until dawn when I was finally released. This would, thankfully, be the last time anything like this would occur!

Heroes are never forgotten but legends never die

Tommy and I managed to work out our issues and I was preparing myself for the third anniversary of the accident.

With the approaching third anniversary of Terry death, I asked Tommy what we should do to commemorate it. He suggested that we do a "Celebrate Terry" event.

I sent some emails and these are what I got in return.

My sister Wanda wrote this:

> *"Terry was an amazing person, a man who was loved, trusted, and respected by all who knew him. He was a man of honor and a man of his word. I have known many men in my lifetime, and I must say that Terry Preas is one of the most amazing! Once your life crossed paths with his, you were never the same.*
>
> *He left a permanent imprint on everyone who met him. When he saw someone in need, he never asked if they needed help, he just met that need without ever expecting anything in return. He was a wise man beyond his years.*
>
> *I miss you Terry and I will forever! But you were not afraid to die, you knew you would be with Jesus and it would be good. He left us before we were ready to let him go but I am forever blessed to have known him."*

From my mother, written in her nearly 90 year old handwriting, just two months before she died.

"Terry was a very proud man, loved and admired by all who knew him. Somehow he touched the lives of all he came in contact with. I am so very proud to have had him for a son in law. Terry was a deeply spiritual man; he believed and practiced these things with his fellow man. He was a wonderful Dad to his two children and a wonderful husband to Kit. I believe Terry was a young genius, solving problems was his expertise.

Rest Terry and God love you. He needed you to mend the chairs behind the Throne for all His loved ones to enjoy."

----*Ma Lucy*

From Tommy.......my future husband

"Terry,

I have given much thought to this letter to you. It was prompted by the anniversary death date and my suggestion to Kit that this date be remembered henceforth as a celebration of your life.

Over a year ago, I answered a computer 'wink' from your soul mate. I see what you saw in her.... a loving and wonderful person with the insight and gumption to stand tall and proud when she remembers you or when things need to be righted. I have become, as you well know, an integral part of her life, and I want to thank you for making her who and what she is today. She makes me look good and I am so proud to stand by her side. But you know all this, because I know in my heart that you had something to do with that 'wink'. The similarities and nuances that constantly arise are proof that your hand was offered to both Kittie and I and you gave us the gentle nudge to push us together. My 'thank you' seems so shallow for all the wonder you have instilled in me. Kittie took me to 'your valley' and I saw the beauty and majesty with my own eyes. She pointed out all the hard work you did with your own hands, the buildings, and the artwork in the gates, fences and all the things that are now so much a part of this Bonita Valley. I cleaned your welding shop and found 'treasures' you made out of raw iron and steel. To say you were an artisan just scratches the surface and does not do you justice. I saw the true inner skills and abilities of a man I wished I could have known in person. That would have made me a better person. More so I have learned of your true legacy by talking and listening to your friends and family members.

You would be so proud of your son, daughter and granddaughter. They are so blessed to have had a Dad like you. I learned the true meaning of a father, a mentor, a confidant, a hunting partner and craftsman. All speak of you with a fond and respectful voice because they knew the true 'you' personally. I had to learn about 'Terry' from their stories and tales from the memories they treasure. I am in awe!

I have come to love the 'love of your life'. I want you to know that I gladly accept the gift you gave me...your Kittie. I thank you for all the wisdom and character you nurtured in her. She can stand on her own two feet and hold her own with anyone. I assure you that I will care for 'your treasure', not to worry about her future...and Trinity, your granddaughter; she is also in good hands...my promise to you. Each time I see your handiwork you left in this valley, I will think of you and all the gifts you left behind. I only wish I could have shook your hand in person and been able to call you my 'friend'."
Tommy

From A.J.

"I am not sure where to start in saying how sad I am to see Terry's life come to pass so quickly. He was one of the most honorable and honest men I've ever known in my life as well as one of the most compassionate and understanding. I will always have fond memories of him and his deep fond roots and respect for the land he walked on and God above, and how we all matter to Him even though we may not see it or understand it. Those conversations and wisdom he imparted on me will never be forgotten or lost for the rest of my life.

He said once to me that you were his everything and that he would have done ANYTHING for you in the world to have you happy and be at your side. A.J."

From Bob Barnhill/Merry Starr Ranch/Sonoita

"Where to begin? I wanted to send this when I heard about Terry's accident. However, I just could not put anything down that made sense. As I wandered around the ranch this past week, I was constantly reminded of Terry's presence. The fences we built, the indoor arena he built, the extensions off some of the buildings that he built, even some of the temporary jigs he used in building these structures are still here. The Ramada area at the Fairgrounds also brings back good memories of him. Terry was a good friend and the memories of all of us at the Buckskin over the years that I owned it will never be forgotten. Still have many pictures of those times.
---BOB"

Things Important To Terry That We Talked About

"A hug from a faithful wife.
Love from honorable children.
A handshake from an honest man.
The security and support from Family and Friends.
The smell of coffee coming from a well made home.
The setting of the sun over the mountains.
The rising of a full moon over a calm lake.
The way his heart would skip a beat when he saw a great buck.
The rise of a covey of quail...
Or the landing of a large fish.

Also this word from family and friends: "Terry Great Job!"

So as a family member and even more important as a friend I say, "Terry, a job well done"."

From Wilber
2003

That was given to me by Terry's cousin and fishing partner, who died in November 2006 from cancer.

I had made these notes from my heart.

Things I miss about Terry

Doing the "Texas Two Step" with him.
His sense of humor.
His encouraging words and attitude.
The way he always made me feel everything would be okay.
His wisdom.
"We'll make it"
His whistling...all the time.
His bear hugs.
"I love ya 'ol gal"
"Things just have a way of working out"
"Man made it, man can fix it"
Coffee time
Table visiting
His "can do" attitude

One of his best friends Paul Taylor wrote:

"Terry had the qualities and personality that money could never buy.
Being able to call him a true friend always made my day and he always
showed true concern for everyone that he met or worked with. My life has a
void in it that was left by Terry's death and I hope in some way I can impart
some of the kindness and friendship that he showed towards me, to others. He
left big shoes for us to fill and for those of us that are still here, the knowledge
and example of how to do it."

My brother R.C.

"Terry was an easy person to love and appreciate because he never changed.
He was always so plausible and kind natured. I never saw him angered, it
seemed like he'd just chuckle when I'd have been throwing stuff. He was
always so soft spoken and considerate, it is so easy to see how he'd become the
gentleman of the community, and loved and respected by so many. If he'd run
for public office in his community, he'd most likely been elected to the post of
his choosing. He was a really genuine person, and those, we don't have nearly
enough of. He was real and can never be dismissed as though he never
existed. Terry left a legacy behind that can be remembered and respected just

like John Wayne! We'll think of him often and fondly, but we'll never remember him outside of his wonderful character."

Terry with Mt Graham in the background

All these words meant so much to me. I knew they were more than just words.

We went back to Bonita that weekend and my intent was to say goodbye to Terry, as I started on the journey of a new love. Every time we went back, there were the pink roses on the white rose bush, as a reminder to me that he was still with me. However, on the weekend of the third anniversary of his death, there were no pink roses. I was an emotional mess and very upset when I didn't see any pink roses. I knew though, that this meant that Terry knew it was time and that I would be okay. I do believe that he hand-selected Tommy for me from Heaven, and he knew when the time was right for him to finally rest. Still it was very difficult for me.

I wrote this letter to him that weekend.

"May 28, 2006
Three long years later

My Dearest Terry,

Three years ago today you left me. While certainly not by choice. the void and emptiness has been the same. I have tried many times to join you, but I guess it just simply isn't my time. I will never understand why God decided it was YOUR time instead of mine! You certainly contributed much more to this world than I, and you surely could have survived much better without me than I have without you!

The best way I know to explain it is that it has been HELL! I have been sad, angry, lonely, sad, angry, lonely, lost, angry, bewildered, angry and sad and lonely and then back and forth all over again. Everything you and I worked for and stood for has gone away, except for the legacy you left in this valley, and that will fade a bit, yet always stay a burning memory, brighter for some than others.

I know that many times since you left, I have let you down, please forgive me, I have made many mistakes but I am still here! I am still living and I have learned to love again. Certainly the youthful love you and I had for each other will never come again, but the love I have found is wonderful, even though it is different than what you and I had. Nothing nor anyone can ever capture my heart like you did; that heart of that young blonde girl, whom you fell in love with at first glance. The life that you and I had was a roller coaster ride, up and down, through valleys and hills and mountains, but they brought us together and then pushed us apart and then brought us back together again and showed us and others that love, true love, can survive most anything if there is a will to do so.

You have, I believe, hand selected my Tommy for me and so now the time has come that I have to say goodbye to you, to let you go and rest, knowing that I will be okay.

Even though I sometimes have my doubts about that, I know that you must feel a peace about it or else your spirit would not have left here and I would have at least one pink rose this day. Instead I have only the sweet fragrance of the love we had, and while I see you everywhere, you seem so far away. Our granddaughter was here today for the first time, and there were moments when I was certain that you and she were having a private conversation. She was looking at you; you were talking to her and making those faces at her, your love for her shining in your eyes.

There is much yet to be done and I know that you expect me to do it. I came home this weekend of your third years passing to say goodbye to you, to ask for your permission for me to heal and to completely live and love again. Once I know that permission is given, maybe I can let go of the past to some extent and go and live the life that you have laid out before me.

Please know that the love you and I had for each other was so special that it can never be totally replaced. I miss you with each step and with each breath but I know it is time for me to tell you goodbye and to set you free to rest now.

I hope that someday I will meet you in Glory and one day I will be with you again, and Tommy will join us there, my two blessings.

I must say goodbye now. It is time for me to live and for you to rest. I love you darlin' and I always will. Thank you for loving me and for helping me become the person I am today.

You can go now. Rest in peace my love. I hope you will meet me where the river forks.
Eternal love,
Your Kit

After I wrote that letter, I emailed a copy of it to my friend Terry aka "Terry 2", as he had been encouraging me to move forward. I was shocked beyond belief the next morning when I opened my email and found this from him, uniquely written as though it was from MY Terry. It sounded just like him. It read....

You know Kit, the time was long overdue. You have worried me many times as to whether you would be strong enough to weather the storms. I would have welcomed you into my arms, but the time was not right. There are lessons on this earth that have to be learned before eternity begins. I would not have left you alone by choice, but would have carried you through your frailties throughout your life. Be strong Kit, but let your good common sense rule your emotions-not the other way around. I know you were angry and I know your sadness. I understand your emptiness and frustrations. The memories cannot be taken away but were meant to be just that--memories of things past, not something to be lived and relived.

Every day is a new day to be taken with renewed strength and your smile to brighten everyone else's day.

You have been sad too long. I am still here. Enjoy the beauty given in life and when death comes in due time-- welcome it then and smile again.

It is not our decision as when is the right time. We are only to accept. Death is not one of the things in life we can change. My contributions to earth were done and my services no longer needed there.

We had a little piece of Heaven in that valley we called home. Let the children play there again. Let their little voices float in the air. Let joy be heard in the valley again.

------ Terry

I was touched beyond belief!

Memory is a way of holding onto things you love,
the things you are, the things you never want to lose

The next month, in June 2006, Tommy told me he wanted to meet my Mother. She was 89 years old and had been widowed for 13 years. She had been on oxygen for a number of years and lived in Texas with her companion of 12 years. She had worried about me so much after Terry's death. Tommy just felt like we needed to go see her.

So we took a flight into Dallas/Fort Worth and visited with brothers and sisters, and then drove on down to meet my mom. She seemed to like Tommy immediately, and vice versa. During the visit, Tommy told her not to worry about me anymore, that he would take care of me. He also told her that one of these days he was going to marry me. Not long after that visit, Mother told my sister that she wouldn't worry about me anymore; she knew I would be okay. It was only about six weeks later that Mother became very ill and hospitalized. It was during that hospitalization that tests showed she had cancer, not only in her lungs but in most of her organs. It was very advanced and the fluid would not stay out of her lungs. Within three weeks she was gone. I was so thankful that Tommy had insisted that we go to see her and that he got to meet her!

On July 15 of 2006, Tommy and I were invited to a barbeque at his friend's house.

There were a number of people there whom neither of us knew.

After we ate, they decided to do Karaoke in the garage. I despise Karaoke because you have to sit through all the bad singers to get to the one good one. When Tommy's friend asked him to come up and sing, I thought "why in the world is he doing this? He never does this." I was even more appalled when I was told I was supposed to go up there and sit on a stool and let him sing to me. I resisted but they insisted so I went. He chose the song "Good Morning Beautiful". He was singing it to me. As soon as he got done singing, he stood in front of me and dropped to one knee and took my hand and said over the microphone "I love you Kittie Preas, I can't live without you, will you marry me?" I was shocked! I never expected it. My response was a quick kiss and "I thought you'd never ask". On the way home that night, he said "that WAS a yes, wasn't it?" I was glad that I got to tell my mom before she passed away.

Tommy and I talked about when and where we wanted to be married. We both wanted a small wedding. I had never had a wedding ceremony as Terry and I had just gone to a Justice of the Peace. We talked about having a judge perform the ceremony, but that seemed too impersonal and besides, I wanted to be married by a minister.

We had definitely agreed on a date of November. In August while Tommy was attending a class for a few days, I decided one day to see if I could try and find an old friend of mine and Terry's from Tucson who used to sell welding rod to us. We knew him as "Jim" and he had become a good friend to us. Jim was a devout Christian.

I searched on the Internet for some possible numbers; I made a few phone calls and left a few messages, along with some apologies to folks who sounded too old to be the Jim I was looking for. I finally got a young voice and so I left a message that if this was the Jim that knew Terry and Kittie Preas from Bonita, would he please call me at my number, which I left. It wasn't too long until he called. I asked him if he knew about Terry, and his reply was "no". As I told him about Terry's accident and death, it was difficult as I knew it was a lot of information in a short time. We had lost contact with him and his family about twenty years prior. Finally in the conversation, I asked how his family was and what was new with him. He told me that he and his son ran a repair business for welding machines but that he had also become an ordained minister and had his own small church over on the east side of Tucson. I couldn't believe my ears! I told him then that while I realized that he had been given a whole lot of information, I had more to tell him. Then I told him about Tommy and that we were getting married in the fall but wanted to be married in a church and by a man of God. I asked him if it was okay with Tommy, would he perform the ceremony in his church. He said he would be most honored! I felt this was more of that "divine intervention".

When I asked Tommy about it, he was thrilled and felt that it was the right thing to do.

We talked about who would escort me down the aisle. I would have loved to have had my son do it but he wasn't able. Suddenly it came to mind to ask a best friend of mine and Terry's who had grown to love Tommy. I talked it over with Tommy and he thought it was a grand idea. So I called our friend Mike and he said he "would be honored!"

I shopped for a dress. My how difficult this was! All the dresses it seemed were geared for the younger generation. Clearly I had lost some weight and when I finally found the right dress, I tried it on and decided if I didn't gain an ounce before the wedding, I would be okay!!It was perfect!

Tommy invited his mom, from Florida, and sister and her husband from Illinois and they agreed to come.

Two of my sisters were coming. I was elated! On what would have been Terry's 54th birthday, Tommy and I went to get our marriage license. We chose this date intentionally. It would bring a happy meaning to what had been a sad day.

I told Tommy he needed a western jacket. He said he didn't have one but asked me if Terry had one. I answered "yes he had two." They were the same size and so I asked Tommy if he would mind wearing one of Terry's jackets. He said "I would consider it an honor." What an amazing man I was marrying!!!

The day approached and I was filled with anticipation. I had asked my daughter to sing at the ceremony, the song "I Could Not Ask For More". The song we had chosen for me to walk down the aisle to was by Celine Dion. It was "The Color of My Love". Absolutely perfect!!

We picked up family at the airport. I could not help but sing the songs "Get me to the Church on Time" and "Going to the Chapel". My heart was so full!!!

That day, my sisters Wanda and Karen and I left early so I could get my hair done and then head over to the church to get dressed. I had kept my wedding dress a secret from Tommy. My hair was beautiful. I glowed with happiness!

The moment arrived.....the church doors opened; I was on Mike's arm as he asked me "Do you know how a monkey in a cage feels now?" The crowd stood in the church for the grand entrance of the bride. I saw my groom standing at the altar. He had tears in his eyes. I had tears in my eyes. I thought "I will not cry!" as we proceeded down the aisle.

When we got there and Mike gave my arm to Tommy, my future husband said to me "Baby you took my breath away!"

We had written our own wedding vows. Each time I would ask Tommy what he had written he would say "2-4-6-8- who do we appreciate? Yeah Kittie!!!"

When it was time, the pastor intended to say "Tom and Kittie, marriage is not to be entered into without ....." Instead he said "Tom and Terry"....... Tommy and I just looked at each other and smiled.....Terry was with us, looking over us, and smiling in approval. Pastor Jim never realized what he had said.

As it became time for us to recite our vows, Pastor Jim read mine to Tommy that I was to recite. I was emotional and had problems talking. I was determined I would repeat those vows!!! They read "Tommy, You are God's precious gift to me: my springtime, my hope and my joy. You are everything that's good and pure and true, and I love you with my mind, body and soul. How blessed I am to be able to say that you are mine, to be able to love and cherish you, for the rest of my days. I vow to always put you first in my life, always be there to comfort you in your sorrow, and rejoice with you in your victories. May our hearts and very breath become one as we unite this day as husband and wife. I promise to be your true love from this day forward and forevermore."

I kept telling myself the tears would not flow, but they did; tears of joy... and tears with so many other emotions.

It was now time for Tommy to recite his vows to me. He and Pastor Jim had conspired against me and planned the "2-4-6-8...who do we appreciate!"

And then "On this special day, Kittie, I give to you in the presence of God and these witnesses, my promise to stay by your side, in sickness and in health, in joy and in sorrow, as well as through good times and the bad. I promise to love you in times of distress, encourage you to achieve all your goals, laugh with you and cry with you, grow with you in mind and spirit, always be open and honest with you, and cherish you, for as long as we both shall live. I give you willingly my heart, my soul and all my love for now and forever".

We sealed ours vows with a kiss, turned and were announced as "Mr. and Mrs. Thomas Koukalik" as we walked back down the aisle. We hugged friends and family, signed the marriage license and then went out the door of the church where an awesome photo was taken of us with bird seed flying through the air. My new life had begun. The question was "could I let go of the previous one?"

Tommy & Kittie wedding kiss

The next day as family left to go back to their homes and Tommy and I prepared to leave for our honeymoon cruise on the following day, my heart was so full, that I could not contain my emotions. I had a wonderful new husband, new life, and another chance at love and I was so thrilled to have had my sisters and my new Koukalik family at the wedding!

Two days after our wedding was also my 53rd birthday. We flew out of Phoenix to Los Angeles and boarded a Royal Caribbean Cruise ship "Vision of the Seas". Even though Southwest Airlines lost our luggage, we had a wonderful honeymoon! Tommy had never been on a cruise, this was my 4th one and I was happy to show him the ropes.

In Puerto Vallarta, we swam with the Dolphins; we got to ride on their stomachs. We had so much fun and so many laughs. We became known on the ship as "the honeymooners who had no luggage". Folks knew it had been found when we had a change of clothes on!

We had a wonderful honeymoon! My heart was so full that at times I thought it would burst!

When we got home, I began the task of changing my name on legal documents. I changed it on the Drivers License, Social Security Card, banking, and we wrote out new wills. It was in black and white, I was Mrs. Koukalik!!! I loved this man who had saved me from the sea of grief and loneliness and believed then and would come to believe stronger as time went on, that Tommy was Heaven sent to me by both God and Terry.

It was approaching time for our annual Bonita Community Bar B Que. It was also the 4th anniversary of the weekend we had Terry's Memorial Service. We talked about what to do and we came up with this idea as noted on the invitations.

JOIN IN A CELEBRATION OF LIVING

THE LIFE THAT I HAD WITH TERRY ENDED 4 YEARS AGO ON MAY 28TH AND A NEW LIFE FOR ME BEGAN ON NOVEMBER 3, 2006 WHEN I COMMITTED TO SHARE THE REST OF MY LIFE WITH TOMMY KOUKALIK.

PLEASE JOIN OUR FAMILY IN SHARING THE WONDERFUL MEMORIES OF TERRY PREAS, AND CELEBRATING THE NEW LIFE THAT I HAVE BEGUN.

WE WILL BE HAVING A "VALLEY BACKYARD CELEBRATION" SATURDAY MAY 26TH AND WOULD LOVE TO HAVE YOU SHARE THIS TIME WITH US...

MEET TOMMY AND OUR GRANDBABY, TRINITY LYNN, NAMED FOR HER PAPA, TERRY LYNN.

We had a good crowd, perhaps some folks came out of curiosity, but I was more than happy to introduce my wonderful husband, Tommy, to them! It was awesome! It appeared to me that there were more of Tommy's friends there than mine and Terry's.

Tommy had made me a beautiful oak chest and had branded Terry's

TEE PEE brand into the top of it. It was a "memory chest" for the purpose of the kids and me placing certain items of our choosing, items that were Terry's. So while the meat was cooking, we did that. It was a very moving and yet meaningful time for all three of us.

As Tommy's friends asked to see the shop, and he proudly showed them, I realized that it was kind of like a "changing of the guards". Old life out, new one in. It was indeed bittersweet!

I wish I could say the transition was easy for me, but in truth, it wasn't! I struggled so much with my new identity. Terry Preas had been in my life for so very many years, and was so much a part of who I was, the person whom I had become! It took me a long time to realize that these feelings were OKAY, normal and that they would pass, in the transition of my new life. Thank God that Tommy was very patient!

Written 12-06-2011

Precious memories, how they linger, how they ever flood my soul. In the stillness of the midnight, precious sacred scenes unfold.

Standing at the kitchen sink in the country this morning, snapping green beans to freeze...a thousand pictures and memories flashed through my mind.

In early 1980 we had returned from a very long trip to Texas and Terry told me we were going to build a home. I told him he was crazy because only wealthy folks built new homes! I went along with him to appease him and he made it happen. On our 9th anniversary he gave me the keys to our new brick home!

Our kids were almost three and six years old. This is the "Bonita Home" where we raised our children, made memories, both good and bad, until God called him home in 2003.

I remember the first year I was emotionally able to put up our Christmas tree. I was already married to Tommy.

As we gingerly pulled out ornaments, there were ones that the kids had made when they were small, the fragile glass ball with glue glitter "Scott, 1980" from kindergarten, that I have guarded for so many years....ornaments Terry and I bought on trips we made in later years. I unwrapped something, and just sat on the couch and cried as I held it. It was a Tupperware melon baller. Tommy couldn't figure out what was wrong with me. I couldn't stop crying. Finally I gained enough composure to tell him the story behind it.

In the '70's, Terry was farm labor. We had sick kids, little money...no dollar stores or Wal-Mart back then. We had spent our money to fly his mom out for Christmas. When we started decorating our tree, we realized just how few ornaments we had. So we went to the kitchen cabinets and got jar rings, the melon baller I had gotten for giving a Tupperware party and other kitchen gadgets to hang on our tree. We didn't have the hanging wires so Terry made some out of bailing wire.

Years later when times were better, we decided to keep the melon baller to hang it on our tree each and every year to remind ourselves of more humble times. I wept.

Our son was sent to a special school when he was 15. Every year when Terry, Becca and I would decorate the tree, Terry would say, (we could count on it)... "I wish Son was here". One time I said "There will come a time you will say "I wish the kids were here". That came to pass, but I never thought there would come a time the kids and I would say "I wish Dad was here".

This afternoon Tommy (my love) and I will pull out all those memories once again and decorate the tree for our grandchild to come for Christmas. Tommy put up the big lighted Christmas star that Becca and her Dad always did together.

I will probably cry when the melon baller is unwrapped. That's ok. Tommy will probably cry with me.

I ask Tommy last night if he ever feels that he is walking in another man's shoes. He said "yes". I asked if it bothers him. He smiled, weepy, and said "No, because I love him too".

The other night we watched a segment of the Waltons where they had planned to build a home on the mountain and leave the family home. In the middle of the night Olivia got up and was sitting in the kitchen, all the memories of raising her family going through her mind.

That's often the way I feel when I come back home, and I guess that's okay. Precious memories, both old and new, how they linger... "

When the heart grieves over what is has lost, the spirit rejoices over what it has left
Sufi Epigram

And so it began...my new life as Mrs. Koukalik. I was now Tommy's wife instead of Terry's wife. Identity is such a complex thing. Being married so young in my life, I never really felt that I became my own person...always someone's wife...someone's mom or someone's widow. It was a very tumultuous time in my life.

I had gone from being a welder's wife, to being a cop's wife, a military wife (Tommy retired from the USAF after serving for 34 years (CMSgt). I also climbed on the back of a beautiful Honda Goldwing motorcycle and rode with Tommy, loving it. I found myself in a Corvette... I went from country life, to part time city life.

My how things had changed! It was an adjustment to say the least.

Never the less, I pressed on. I think maybe a part of me thought that I did not deserve to have TWO such wonderful men in my life! However I can say that these two loves have been extremely different. The love of our youth is special and yet...the love of our mid-life takes on a different specialty...not better...no worse...just different and different is ok. The love that I have for Tommy is just as intense as that young love I had for Terry. I am thankful for Tommy's patience and understanding, his undying devotion to me, our marriage, his respect for Terry's memory and to my emotional health. He is truly a blessing in my life.

Tommy has now retired, and we are planning to move back to the country home. The home that Terry and I built and raised our children in. The home where love once lived, and now love will live again.

And I am going to have another grandchild!

Was it an easy journey? Absolutely not...but so worth the trip!!!

Life goes on if we let it.

EPILOGUE

It is now several years since Terry's accidental death. I have been away for a week.

I realize that I am so very anxious to return to Tommy, my Tommy and our life together. It is a certain sign that I have healed! The memories of Terry and the life that we had are just that...memories. ...warm and precious. No one can ever take them away from me. They comfort me and make me smile but I realize on this return trip from Texas that Tommy completely has my heart.

I am blessed once again to love and be loved by a magnificent man. We have a wonderful life together, to which I am anxious to return.

He meets me at the jet way, one dozen pink roses in hand! We embrace in a warm and loving hug. I am home!

How can I keep from singing?

 Kittie Preas Koukalik was born in Texas and moved with her young husband, Terry, to the Bonita AZ area in 1973. In 1982, Terry started Preas Welding.

It was there they raised two children.

Today Kittie lives in the family home with her new husband, Tommy; they have one granddaughter and are planning for the birth of their second.